THE BEST
NEW BRITISH
AND IRISH
POETS
2019-2021

CO-JUDGED BY
NICK MAKOHA
AMIRA GHANIM
EDITED BY
AMIRA GHANIM

THE BEST
NEW BRITISH
AND IRISH
POETS
2019-2021

THE **BLACK SPRING**
PRESS GROUP

First published in 2021
by Eyewear Publishing Ltd / Black Spring Press Group
Suite 333, 19-21 Crawford Street
Marylebone, London W1H 1PJ
United Kingdom

Cover design and typeset by Edwin Smet
Printed in England by TJ Books Ltd, Padstow, Cornwall

Series editor Todd Swift
*The Series Editor would like to thank Edwin Smet for the particular time
and care he has taken in typesetting this complex text.*

ISBN 978-1-912477-70-8

BLACKSPRINGPRESSGROUP.COM

Dedicated to
Leah Fritz

TABLE OF CONTENTS

7

PREFACE BY AMIRA GHANIM

Welcome to this double-sized anthology of poets, selected over two years by Nick Makoha and myself. The idea behind this book, based on the famous American series, is to discover and showcase some of the finest British and Irish poets not yet under contract at the time of selection.

We invited poets to submit their poems to a contest in order for the judges to act as editors who select one poem from the entrants that strike them as original, unique, fresh or otherwise significant. Poems have come to us in several welcome waves, including across a pandemic and lockdowns, and capture a sense of diverse perspective. The one hundred poets represent many communities and identities, something we hope can be emphasized more in future publishing, in order to engage with the reality of our times.

This anthology is wonderfully evocative, funny, moving and engaged, and passionate about poetry and the world. We are aware that many of the best poets and poems are still hiding in these isles somewhere, and we hope to come across your work as we continue our search and exploration in future anthologies.

Readers who want to be introduced, in one handy place, to a hundred vital and emerging poets, are likely to be well-served by this anthology. The poems have been blended together, alphabetically by last name, but those wishing to see who each judge picked can look at the appendix in the back.

Finally, we want to thank the poets for their cooperation, enthusiasm, support and patience during a particularly challenging time for all of us — it really has been a pleasure working with each and every one of you and we hope that we have carried your work with great care in this anthology.

INTRODUCTION BY NICK MAKOHA

In reading this year's selection of poems for *The Best New British and Irish Poets* anthology it warmed me to see the risks that the poets were taking. If I led with the heart I could have easily included all the submissions and I found that inspiring. But in accordance with protocol some threshold had to be reached.

Beyond the striking line and turn of phrase what swayed my choice were the poems that could weave a web of words with equal doses of surety and sensitivity. I read all poems at least five times at different times of the day. I wanted to be certain that my differing daily moods did not dull my attention to each poet's craft. I looked for the cumulative effects of musicality, story, form and lyric swing. The poems I have included are those that were able to do this without showing the joins.

All the poems kept my attention and had a static cling. In some ways the titles the poets chose were terraforming language and preparing us for the worlds to come. The poem's first line is the title and here is where a lot of the poems excelled. In my line by line readings I interrogated the narrative impulse and the emotional impulse. Poetry is a simple engine. Words are its fuel. This ancient art-form is an excellent receptacle for story, myth, song and emotion. With such forces it is possible to travel across borders, of time, space, gender. In fact, all membranes become porous.

Poets that intrigued me were the ones who understood that what is remembered and what is imagined are part of the same continuum. I looked for poems that gave off a certain kind of heat or moved with a unique velocity such that the perception of the world was altered as I travelled through the poem. I also look for what I call the Tardis effect. This is a poem that can move me across time and emotion without my outward perception. All this is a roundabout way of saying: I was looking for connection. I was looking for poets who could untangle language and reach out across the page. I was looking for poets who supply their own light. Or as Stanley Kubrick said:

The most terrifying fact about the universe is not that it is hostile but that it is indifferent, but if we can come to terms with this indifference, then our existence as a species can have genuine meaning. However vast the darkness, we must supply our own light.

So reader, here is a little bit of light from these isles. I hope you enjoy reading the poems as much as I have liked judging them.

MUHIBO ABDALLA

is 20-years-old and is currently studying
Pharmaceuticals at university. She is from
Leicester and has been published by *Young
Writers*. As the child of refugee parents from East
Africa, Abdalla's poem is based on the region's
history. In her spare time, she helps plan a
local sports group, Imra Active.

14

THE FRACTURED HORN

The one thing that doesn't abide by majority rule is a person's conscience

- To Kill A Mockingbird by Harper Lee

The magnitude of a catalyst becomes the beholder
of discomfort and disdain towards those who ignited the chain reaction.
Deplorable catalysts struck onto humanity inflict an eternal dent on their livelihoods.
Intertwined with those showered on by the Earth's nature of withdrawing from the horn, leaving it depleted and dry.
Calculated catalysts, instilled through imperialistic gains, fleet from the treaty of Versailles.
Fracturing the horn into regions and tribes, distant, our people suffer from these allies.

Fragments of our jewels dispelled across the western globe.
With her slender neck, Nefertiti's beauty fades,
she is an outcast, blinded by their lecherous glares
as her stature erodes, she remains inescapable like a ginger rabbit caught in the headlights.
Their führer wickedly driven by extremes to sever masses of *mishpochas*.
A stagnant treacherous sin which taints the earth's crust, sprouts cyanide to engulf his toxic soul.
The sound of restoration ricochets from the oboe da caccia.

The inevitable torment arises once again.

Mussolini clamours into the forbidden land full of greed and lunacy.
His succession transmogrifies Haile Selassie into a skunk that expunges what is left of the euphony of his land.
Ethiopia now frail like a germinating shoot that has lost its unilateral source of light, withers into quicksand.
Wars upon famines, Abyssinia hangs on its last strand as it plunges Selassie to his retribution.
His remains, befitting to his cumbersome leadership, lay sprawled across the unsanitary corners of the imperial palace.
Their vile actions foredoom their rightful end, their civilians callous to the wasteland they left.

Pain is the root, the stem, the burst which alights an individual to commit a heinous crime.
Nature's gift of a palatial coast envelopes a shoal of fish, this sublime beauty, stolen for their personal gain.
Again, the horn of Africa is left to gnaw on dirt so as to silence their bellies, hopeful the colonisers won't return.
Like a stinging wasp they return with their grand fishing nets, causing the fishes to squirm and writhe.
The outcome, a generation of pirates who carry out nefarious reprisals only to provoke their own unforgivable demise.

The power of love may restore the deteriorated horn.
The antidote so eagerly sought out, scavenged along every surface of the horn
remains easily accessible, like the keratin which strengthens the pronghorn.
Forgiveness, a noble act yet burdensome for the piercing cyst engraved within the heart's septum
carries the infinite agony felt for generations.
Though the cast of Anteros strokes their hearts, they forgive but never forget.

Civil wars flare from intolerances inducing divisions in the barren land.

Our bodies stitched, silenced from the uprising, we are numb to all desires.

The men plough to sew our garments so that they hang ill-fitted against our bodies like an extinguished wildfire billowing to the minute gusts of air, painting us as cakes that puff and de-puff.

Like a Mediterranean octopus we are visibly shapeless, with stationary garments, a shield from the ominous voyeurs.

How deluded are you to perceive us as *oppressed?*

Libertà.

The east of Africa once united through the fusion of their language, their people, their musical harmonies.

Alike were their oppressors, but together they forgave and cleansed the horn of all deformities.

Now the oppressors wait anxiously, fearful for our retributive action.

Awoken, with blazingly hazy, tireless eyes.

Our queen bee situates herself nonchalantly amongst them, custodial of her hive yet fearless to sting if they strike again.

Here I pray that a catalyst is no more, wishfully reciting *amen.*

PETER ADAIR

lives in Bangor, Northern Ireland.
His poems have appeared in *The Honest
Ulsterman, PN Review, The Galway Review,
Poetry Ireland Review, The Bangor Literary Journal,*
and elsewhere. In 2016, Adair won the Funeral
Services Northern Ireland poetry competition,
and in 2018, two of his poems were shortlisted
for the Seamus Heaney award for new writing.
'The Acorn Road' first appeared in *PN Review*.

THE ACORN ROAD

That chilly morning a soldier dug a grave,
lowered down his mate and laid a wreath at the wall
of the garden. I stopped, too far off to see

if he wept, then pushed the wheelbarrow full
of acorns – thousands of acorns – to sow
in neat raised beds in a polytunnel.

Beyond the trees arose a general's chateau
behind their lines. I passed my great-uncle by chance
beside the willow cuttings in serried row

on row like gravestones in a field in France
forever Ulster. And creeping from tents
in Clandeboye, bricklayers, sons of the manse,

clerks, still in civvies, fired German rifles
at the birdie while gunshots resounded
in the woods – guests slaughtering partridges.

We buried the acorns, named the ridge Acorn Road,
as they might call their trenches homely names:
Sandy Row, Markethill: names spelt in blood.

Nearby, three lads sat at a rusty table
and played cards, chatted, as if they'd never left
this land. I walked over. We had so much to say,

so much, but the next moment they were lost
to sight, and the workless boy pushed a roller
over the Acorn Road to smooth the compost.

Later, I watched the soldiers march down darkened lanes
to another land, and gable murals on new estates.

CAROLINE AM BERGRIS

is a member of the Pitshanger Poets Collective
in London. Am Bergris is a physically and
mentally disabled woman who has, as the poet
herself writes, spent 3 months living on the
streets of London and had to flee to a domestic
refuge in fear of her life. She won the Over
The Edge Poetry Prize Competition and has
been published in various journals in Europe
and America. Am Bergris is set to have a book
published in 2021 (Marble Poetry).

BEFORE MORPHINE

Tsunamis begin with drawback
pain receding,
teasing with its absence –
only the frothing surface warns.
      Then the rising wall heaves forward,
      agony smashing through barricades of pills,
      ripping off roofs.
            Legions of spasms surge,
            carrying the smell of affliction –
            medicine, sewage, blood.
                  The throbbing percussion of pain
                  beats you into the underworld
                  whilst you are silent, courage submerged.

Even when the destruction is finished
and you survey what survives,
the debris, the skeleton of pain
still hurts –
a reluctant
      pang,
a relic.

ANGELA ARNOLD

has been published in various UK poetry magazines including *Magma*, *Dream Catcher*, *Popshot*, *Anima*, *Marble*, *OWP*, *The Journal* and *The Interpreter's House*, in addition to several anthologies. As well as being a poet, Arnold is a painter, writer of non-fiction and a creative gardener. She is currently learning the Welsh language.

THE KNOWLEDGE OF SILVER

It's not dirt, you babble, emphatic,
hastily swipe something aside
with a gesture: not dirt.
I know.

The wintry coat the kettle grows and
*re*grows, flakes as you tip; rimes and prime
stain grabbers – tea a speciality, and
spoons that will sport half trans-ethnic moons

all round the rim, whitely silver still
inside. I know what it takes: a sharp
fingernail to groove away,
stubbornly, scourers

only leaving that unspoon smell
of pungent newness –
inappropriate.
But you, you don't scrape, scrape,

scrape; you're content
that all is as should be,
intact, underneath and really,
I would think, maybe

as a husband might
still walk heavy footed,
most midnights,
to the perfect drum of your pulse.

22

CYNTHIA ASARE-DOMPREH

is a qualified Occupational Therapist, and has worked in the field of Mental Health for 20 years. She was born in Ghana and is a mother of three. Asare-Dompreh hopes to utilise her poetry and prose as part of the healing process where generational trauma is present, and advocates for those whose voices have been silenced, unheard or simply ignored.

CONVERSATIONS WITH MY SON

When my son got to such a height that he could

look me straight in the eyes,

and I knew now the world

would see him as a threat,

as a sexual predator,

or an aggressor,

I warned him.

My son,

unless you're entertaining or serving,

there are only a few other places society

wants to see a black male like you.

In prison

falsely accused of rape,

In a mental institution,

or in your grave

24

ROBERT BAL

is a poet of the South Asian diaspora and
and is currently a visitor on Squamish,
Musqueam and Tsleil-waututh First Nations
land in North America. His poem is from
Protection, a collection that explores growing up
as a male-coded person of colour in London,
England, in the aftermath of the colonial
experience, along with the consequences of
paternal abandonment, psychological patriarchy,
and life in the age of late stage capitalism.

DEATH, A VALLEY

you can hear it in the echo of the unlit passage underground always
coming through. it whispers now and now and now and now, and as
the floorboards sway you think to yourself, yeah, that's it, that's all the
way i'm in it, but the two of you haven't met before, and you aren't
meeting now, because how's a self inside it go again?

all the pressure of our practiced metropolitan desire, the gravid
always moment of our single rareness, split for seconds to never stop.
we get reconvened and filled. we wreck in wonder at the way it comes
inside defeat, the paraontological, the teargas moment when we know
we've been secure, but now we're out there and defenceless, pushed
out through the frame to fall, all formless, and damned to always fail
to land.

we've been preformed to have to hand the self back. that's the hardest
stake we get to carve. the impact of it driving in is one from two,
unscarred and recombined, come back to itself but gone from sight,
and that's alright, because i'm not backing out now. i might as well
look forward to it. all these words i trawl for it catch nothing but love.
when you look for me and you can't find me, look for me out on the
verge. come join me when it's time.

KRYSTELLE BAMFORD

was born in France and raised in the US. She
currently lives in Scotland with her partner
and two kids. Her poetry has appeared in
The American Poetry Review, *bath magg*, *Under
the Radar*, *The Scores*, in addition to several
anthologies. Bamford is a 2019 Primers (Nine
Arches Press) poet, and is the recipient of the
Scottish Book Trust New Writers Award, along
with being shortlisted for the Bridport Prize,
the 2020 Oxford Brookes International Poetry
Competition and longlisted for the
2019 National Poetry Competition.

28

MY DAUGHTER'S MY LITTLE PONY

Both war horse and bed horse it heralds snow or a heart shot through and I worry for
it—arabesque, scooped and bright, it looks like a cake before the carving. I was lucky,

empty and preserved, but in our small school there were girls who were
filled, heated to boiling, their lips traced around and

the wells of its hoofprints glitter like shattered flatware or the buried gleaming
of casings on a streambed. I'd like to tell you

about a girl named Erin who glowed like a vacant sun
and Lorie who was haunted like a house not possessed like a person

and this pony, who was branded while still in the caul, all spilled intestine
and clefted plum. These were the girls, mostly but not all poor,

like buckets who caught the rain in the corridors of our school
which was shaped like an E for 'ending' or 'egg' or 'eros'

and from my daughter's bedstand, between the board book and plastic watch, this pony
bends to me, as if it knows it was me who brought it here. *Yearbook '99*:

Jen, most likely to never be seen again; Nicole,
intelligence rusts cut in the rain, then sharpens, and here

its eyes are raised like sails, big with invisible things driving it back—
away from me my daughter this room and while

I know there is happiness there, no less in quality than my own and that girls
become the gorgeous baying bitches of the world, I find myself wishing them all

back to the bloody nest where it lay against the length of its mother
for those minutes, golden and meted, before it was asked to stand.

29

CAROLINE BANERJEE

is a 22-year-old poet from Brighton,
England, recent graduate from the University
of Cambridge, where she read English. She is
currently completing an MA in Medieval Stud-
ies at King's College, London. In 2019, Banerjee
was awarded the T.R. Henn Prize for her po-
etry, and her work was recently commended in
Frosted Fire's 2021 New Voices Competition.

LESSONS

My teacher used to have this rule
That when you were really struggling
To focus, you had to run around the
Whole set of classroom blocks,
And when you came back,
You'd be 'as good as new'.

With only a t-shirt on,
I ran out into the frosty morning,
hooks (white) catching
On my plimsolls,
Cheeks like newly lit fuses.

I return in an instant.
Head pulsing with the air of now.
Only to find an empty classroom,
Morphed plastics,
Desks floating in a bath
of sun.

ALEXANDRA BANISTER-FLETCHER

is currently based in South London, where she is a poet and arts writer. Her work has been published in *The Art Story, HART Magazine,* and *The London Student*.

BIRCH WOOD

Crisp treads, where you were wed
The forest and the glade.
Smoke rose, when night fell
And the red bus looked lost.
Marooned in green, your white shone out
And dazzled in the fire.
On the horizon, I could see
A father with his child.

SARAH BARR

currently teaches writing groups and
leads a Dorset Stanza group. Her poems
have appeared in anthologies and magazines,
including *The Frogmore Papers, The Interpreter's
House, Poems in the Waiting Room, The Mechanics'
Institute Review 2019, Live Canon 2019 Anthology,
Templar Poetry Anthology, The Caterpillar,* and
elsewhere. Barr won the Frogmore Poetry Prize
2015 and The National Memory Day Poetry
Competition 2018. Her pamphlet, *January,* was
published in 2020.

DARTMOOR SNOW

We stride out
and listen to the scrunch of boots
in the deep, dry powder.
Down the slippery path where frosted catkins
and hawthorn overhang
to the half-way metal bench
upholstered in white.
We track across the sloping field,
admire our footprints,
greet the only other human out today,
a swaddled woman with terriers
who roll, pat paws, and turn
into snow-dogs.
We catch snow-flakes on our tongues.
Neige, nieve, sneachta, eira, snaw,
a blurring of boundaries.
The sky thickens
and snow keeps falling.
Where are all the children?
Returning home, a fringe of icicles
hangs from the shed roof eaves.
We play music,
slice bread, pour wine.

AMY BLYTHE

is from Kildare, Ireland. She graduated
from Queens University Belfast with an
MA in Creative Writing, and she has been
published in *The Stinging Fly, Crannóg,
Banshee*, amongst others.

THE WITCH

Sometimes, she would let them see her. She'd walk
right past their houses, step through their gardens, stand
wearing rags on their streets. She'd let them talk,
about the cobwebs she held in her hand,

let them laugh at how she went about life
let them sneer at how she knew she never
wanted to be a mother or a wife
and liked her home cold. Yet, how and ever,

she was raised to welcome all passers-by,
to keep the good cauldrons for company,
though people stopped in less and less to buy
her charms for love and tricks for gluttony.

Let them think her mad, for she was content
to have them miss the threat she aimed to vent.

LEO BOIX

is a Latinx bilingual poet born in
Argentina, who currently resides in the UK. He
has featured in various anthologies, including
Ten: Poets of the New Generation and *Un Nuevo Sol:
New Latinx Writers*. Boix's poems have appeared
in *POETRY, PN Review, The Poetry Review,
Modern Poetry in Translation*, and elsewhere.
He is the recipient of the Keats-Shelley Prize
2019 and is currently a fellow of The Complete
Works Program, as well as the co-director of
'Invisible Presence', a scheme to nurture new
young voices of Latino poets in the UK. *Ballad of
a Happy Immigrant* is his debut English collection
published in June 2021 (Chattus & Windus,
Penguin/Random House).

SEÑOR DE LA NOCHE (LORD OF MANY NAMES)

i-*La mujer*

A door shut, a machete dropped.
   You woke her up with strange noises,
drops of sweat covered her body.
   A hammock nestled her, legs dangling.
Some say you stole her barefoot that night,
   took her deep in the selva. Hypnotist
gaze, your hairy face uncrowned.

They say you forced her. She didn't
   scream enough. You left her abandoned
under a knotted ceiba tree. They talked
   of tainted sperm. Her seven children
ugly as you. They smell alike. Spotted
   fruit for black bees to feed on. Scions
of half-moons. Their monstruos hands.

Lascivious nightjar, your illusive whistle
   echoes all that dies in the forest
a myth no one dares to speak of.
   Your forbidden name, peril hides
in every letter, a sudden call: their pit.
   Believers prefer to name you quietly,
but never—*nunca!* at night.

ii- *El hombre*

39

Will you turn transparent, Pombero
   lure him in, with your obscene dance?
He walked knowing something
   behind infested yataí trees.
They didn't see him as he pleaded,

no witness around. You opened him.
Then escaped into the form of a golden sicalis.

Slumped on dried salty mud, blooming
    pink Lapacho covered in honeyed milk
on his arse. The mark of an ambush
    he could not forget, as he returned
among buttress roots, his swollen eyes.
    As he tasted Pÿragué's saliva,
    a burning hymn on an altar fire.

Instead of coins, they leave you rum,
    fresh tobacco, molasses for you to snatch.
Burning incensed tapers for protection,
    a bad harvest beckons. Drink it all
Karaí Pyhare, you are the poor farmer's saint.
    Instead of eyes, amber stones gleam,
you kneel down, kiss the ground.

iii- *El pueblo*

    Pombero, with just one stroke
you make them go mad, they lose
    all they have—their gods, their demons.
Your hairy palm unlocks the forest door:
    headless animals, babies upside down
hanged from trees, stolen novias in parts.
    Grinning trophies you dangle around.

They say you are lord of a silver mountain,
    that somewhere inland, in the woods,
rises a summit of pure silver—de plata.
    They say you are known to be generous,
that you'd gladly give me part of
    your treasure: a goodwill sign, a talisman,
some feathers. A silvered tongue.

Now that night has fallen, this Sylvan forest
   of yours grows ears, you are back
to bewitch them with your dog whistle,
   your echo of an echo. Beware
of scattered semen, it pollinates the jungle,
   seeds will spread, strangle the shallow floor
until all is spoiled. Cho Pombé's gain.

iv-*La invocación*

You could name all the things inside yourself:
   a Universe going backwards
for a deathless ritual. You'll promise
   to protect all passerine birds that land
on your cracked hand. They'll be good
   to you, Pombero, to your tender outline
if they follow you around: You'll be named.

They now say you roam the forest to save us,
   our thicket, el monte. You will ambush
the insatiable spoilers. Slaughter
   bird-catchers, fishermen, loggers.
If they can't see you, where is your heart?
   Where the wild force that guides you?
Selva's eyes have opened, she woke me up.

Pombero, come close to me. Strip me
   of skin, bones, precious stones
as I invoke you, your unholy tail.
   Furtive figure, no shadow disappears
but footsteps, crushed wet leaves
   suffocate the poisonous dawn.
Then a sudden knock at the door. *There!*

41

JULIE BOLITHO

is a British-American writer and painter
residing in Oxford, England. Her essays have
been recognised by the *Best American Essays*
anthology and her poetry has been published
across multiple platforms internationally. She is
currently writing a memoir and her teachings
can be found through her course, talks and
meditations on the international app, Insight
Timer. www.julieelagrace.com

FLYING IN PAKISTAN'S AIRSPACE

the mountains below look like a pod of whales –
their long spines curving up into the dry heat
as the bows of their heads
dive deep into the thick rock below.

I think of the bones in the mountains,
the millennia of marrow and ash,
how many beings, ancient and formidable,
remain on this earth in particles,
predator and prey melded together
for foreseeable centuries.

There are occasional settlements
pockmarked throughout the pale terrain.
There are days between the villages and I
cannot make out any roads from my perch in the sky –
only small water sources
running gold under the rising sun.

I wonder in what ways these mountain dwellers return
their dead to the Earth.
I wonder if mountains can move
with old heart beats,
how long the body echoes,
and echoes
and echoes.

JIMMY BOWMAN

is a poet and teacher of English,
Media and Film at a state secondary school
in South London, where he grew up on a
working-class estate. Jimmy produces and
presents 'People's Poetry Podcast'.

ONE TOWN MAN

What was the name of that old park?
The one they built the new flats on.
They were built 23 years ago –
he recalls a morning commute
through the ponds
was like landing in Normandy,
a world before 3G and knives
clock the wrong person
and receive black eyes,
the old burgundy blazers
were long gone as his school turned academy,
knowledge is big business now like carpets.

When milk had a man
and a poor excuse of a van
he'd never had stronger bones,
half-inched glass bottles
smashed in the piss hut
glittered through the night
like drum and bass.

Walk with him down the high street
he's a local historian,
That pound shop was Woolies once,
that used to be a Spar,
two bakers on one High Street,
world's gone mad.
He remembers the land that vanished
below the new supermarket
and how the chain restaurants
bullied the local coffee shops,
the small green outside

the job centre now housed an Odeon.
People don't need jobs they need
brightly coloured fabrications
of lives they'll never have.

Before it was a place of worship
congregations of trackies,
sermons led by the older kids
as they sat on bicycles watching
their elders sign on.
That was still more exciting
than any million-dollar
blockbuster.

The same goals stand on different pitches
and the same rivalries divide different
generations.
When did neat vodka turn
into Parkrun? Where did Glen go?
Did he stop being exciting?
Wimbledon was in a cage
metal nets and McEnroe rage,
now the spiders holiday in Racket
and other such youthful relics
lost amongst the various
coloured dustbins –
it's a brave new world.

He can tell you the price of lager
in all five of the local watering holes
but more importantly –
how much it used to be.
There's only one decent boozer here
and you're sitting in it.
He's a walking bus timetable

a greasy spoon connoisseur
he knows anyone who's anybody
and where things occur,
he's an unofficial mayor
a man of the people
he can tell you what and where
as he points to the steeple,
Aren't wedding bells so rare?
He admires the Church for reminding
people of what came before,
he's a blurb on a stone
waiting to be immortalised.

Some scoff at the One Town man
from their Instagram show homes
miles from anyone, likes for their
solitary confinement
but my god was it under the asking price.
He'd take the worn-out streets and misty
apparitions of tomorrow's yesterday
every day, they made him feel
more than any double tapped heart.
They say community is dead but
it's what you put in.
A true home requires
less DIY and more
conversations.

Every bridge has a story, every alleyway a name
some bring laughter, some bring pain,
the derelict houses and washed out shops
peer closely at the One Town man
strolling nonchalantly down memory lane,
unfazed at the modern world
smiling at the memory of what came before –
if nostalgia literally means our pain,
this One Town man didn't feel any.

TERRY BOYLE

is from Northern Ireland, and currently
resides in the USA. He is a retired professor
of English Literature, holding a D.Phil. Boyle
currently writes a monthly column for the
Irish American News in Chicago and Ohio. His
subject matters cover Northern Ireland, and
modernising medieval mystery plays. Boyle's
play *Oh, What a Bloody Good Friday!* reached
the semi-finals in 2011 of the O'Neill
competition and it was later produced
by Loyola University, Chicago.

A NEW ECONOMY

Words, felled in trees, are fast disappearing,
It's the click and mouse game that is the new thing,
Heaven has been sublet to help with rising costs
The man above is to introduce a new marketing scheme,
Angels and archangels must put their collective wings
Together and create a more user-friendly environment,
A new economy, with less pomposity and ceremony,
Will become a virtual revelation of multimedia glory.

Connectivity, composed of interpersonal relations,
Will be phased out in favour of less risky behaviours,
Platforms, created for brief encounters, prove popular,
If you don't mind the gap,
Human interaction is to be contained, minimized,
In the new economy, health and survival are paramount
And, require us to curb the urge to merge.

Plagues are a small price to pay for progress,
We are hosts to demons, due to our curious interactions,
Thankfully, now in sterile spaces, we can explore a web
Of our own making,
The new economy ensures such conveniences are satisfying,
On a cloud of contentment, we will live out our existence,
Heavenly mansions apportioned to us in mega, giga,
Tera, and petabytes,
A mystical place to upload your soul to the great matrix
Where you can ascend and descend in lucid dreams,
But, for now, let not your hearts be troubled, it's all about to
Change.

49

CAROLINE BRACKEN

was selected for the 2018 Poetry Ireland
Introductions Series. Her poems have been
published in *The Irish Times, The Fish Anthology,
The Ogham Stone, Sonder Magazine, Nous Sommes
Paris,* amongst others. One of her poems can
be heard on the Poetry Jukebox at the
EPIC Museum in Dublin.

MIDNIGHT EXPRESS

Did you ever drive out of your life at midnight
down a dark road with your sleeping-bagged children
singing back-seat summer holiday songs
and chattering about crazy-golf and chips and candyfloss
even though Christmas lights still hung on your abandoned tree?

Did you ever have a plan that led you to a safe house
fumble at a stubborn door with an un-turnable key
your worldly goods in a heap at your feet
treasures you were told you would need;
birth-certs, bank cards, social security numbers?

Did you ever bed down reluctant bodies in random rooms
then stand smoking on a stranger's porch
stare at a sky of unfamiliar stars
and thank God for the most precious gift
of a car?

GAVIN BRADLEY

is an Irish writer from Belfast, currently working in Edmonton, Canada. He has been published in *Glass Buffalo, The North, The Caterpillar,* along with anthologies that include *Frozen Fairy Tales* and *Fantastic Trains,* amongst others. Bradley's poetry has been selected for a Hennessy New Irish Writing Award by *The Irish Times.* Instagram: @gavinbradleywrites

HEMINGWAY'S COSMONAUT

In the sixties, a Russian Cosmonaut fell from space.
I imagine him in a soundless swan dive as below,
Bing Crosby crooned on the Marconi,
and Katherine Hepburn was still playing around with chimpanzees;
anachronistic, but I never liked John Lennon or Faye Dunaway.
He fell like a lawn dart and burned up like Sunday Morning bacon.
They put his ashes on display in the Kremlin,
next to the reluctantly taxidermied Lenin,
whose stern face seems to say: "tell me about it".
Then there were these Tibetan monks,
who would wander out onto the slopes peppered with snow
that melted under feet blazing with holy fire,
and mummify themselves, prostrate, for forgotten reasons,
that would only be remembered by Hemingway
who, in the sweet-smelling throws of Cuban rum,
would shoot himself for them, and for all the words he could not touch.
I feel guilty, because I know I would never die for
Tao, or Art, or even the endless Quiet of space.
I might, though, if you asked me to go first,
and see what all the fuss is about.

MATT BROOMFIELD

is a a British poet, journalist and activist
who recently spent three years living and
working in Rojava, North and East Syria, in
solidarity with the Kurdish- and women-led,
direct-democratic revolution. 'Ceasefire' was
written in Rojava, where Broomfield featured in
publications including *Tahoma Literary Review*,
Ink, Sweat and Tears, *Agenda*, *Glass and Argot*,
The National Poetry Society and *The Independent*,
amongst others. His poems have also been
featured in the Poetry On The Underground
series. Broomfield is a former Foyle Young
Poet of the Year.

CEASEFIRE

people want very much to lay out six packets of crisps
and three tins of tomato paste on a small trestle-table
outside their bombed-out house.

they will die for this, laying hands on unexploded mines,
but then they will die if it is not done,
the heart sometimes just stopping,
or otherwise self-immolating, six years later,
in front of the UNICEF offices.

human rights are very large,
hygienic, armour-plated with guarantees:
and almost all will waive them gladly
for the two-foot garden
and the shrubs in old tomato tins.

people want very much to hang up bright pink pairs of socks
between walls still smeared with ash and sometimes blood,
to offer the second-to-last cigarette from a crushed-up packet
to a neighbour not blamed
for the sins of his sons.

and if there are eight families living in one abandoned petrochemical plant,
for sure they will divide the turbine-hall with curtains
and respect one another's space,
and perhaps they will organise themselves
via a committee of sorts,
responsible for sharing out the cooking-oil and gathering the children
to learn to read and write in a minor mother-tongue,

and though the place where they always hung up their socks to dry
has been swallowed by mountainous pain, perhaps they will find

55

that the pain of this is less
if they and their neighbours
do their laundry via rota
and let their two-foot gardens
flow into one long melon patch:
perhaps.

MICHAEL A. BROWN

was born in Manchester, and currently resides in Heaton Moor, England, with his husband and adopted son. Brown is the author of *The Exhibit; Mercurial* and *Meet Me At The Harbour.*

THE ADOPTION

Stage 1

Wondering if you've been born
as we fill in blanks on forms

Under the microscope
we squirm like new life forming

Stage 2

An intensive and intrusive job interview for becoming
parents
the panel allocate 'links'

Playing with traumatised children at activity days
we hope to be matched

Stage 3

We wait six months for your birth certificate
you're finally crowned with your new double-barrelled
surname

You read the letter to your future self
and now call me Dad

IAN CAPPELLI

is from Ireland and is an MFA candidate
at George Mason University. He is the author
of *Suburban Hermeneutics,* and his current,
forthcoming publications include *Roanoke
Review, Watershed Review, The Menteur,* and
High Shelf Press, amongst others. 'BODHI
CHRISTMAS: JANUARY' was published
in *Enizagam.*

59

BODHI CHRISTMAS: JANUARY

I confine my Zen garden
ornaments in cardboard, while
listening to the neighbors' slack-
jawed impressions of Elvis,
crooned from across the snow,

and decide that I will fold the i-
Tunes gift card my mother gave
me eight times, until it knows it
is nothing.

> Elvis is dead,
> *Blue Christmas is over.*

I mute the first *Alien* film, and
hear people weeping under
their trees. There was another
massacre in a crowded place.
My rice packet is almost done.

I fail at becoming a chopstick
Jazz drummer while the now
muted movie continues. Samsara
is kind of like New Year's Eve.
People are really sad about
the massacre.

> For a moment,
I forget about rebirth.

> Never mind.

I unmute the movie at the part
where it is unclear whether
or not there is a main character
other than the alien.

FINN CARGILL

was born in Suffolk, England, and he has since lived in Glasgow and London. He is a student of Media and English at Goldsmiths College, and currently works at a community cinema. Cargill curates the collaborative project 'Dirty & Anxious' with fellow poet Luke Surl, housing creators from different artistic backgrounds. Website: finncargill.com Instagram: finn.cargill // dirty_and_anxious

DAYS OF MERCY

I strangled my broken memory of a horse
Into a clod of potter's clay and painted it poorly,
Victory Red when wet – now a dry, spiced mud.
The lodgers eat their potatoes without salt,
One fries onions in the bottom of the kettle.
I, their idiot father, inhale the fat in the air,
Heavy, massaging my bread-and-beer gut.
Today I was a sun dog, waiting restlessly to rise
And alongside my mother, puncture the sky.
Though my cue never came. Hurt,
Like the paunched rabbit hung up
Before me, I watched my blue entrails
Thud onto the wood-effect vinyl flooring.
My surrogate Turk aunt at the corner shop warned me
Of the dangers of painkillers in times like these.
I explained, it's only for the bulging pain behind my eye
That brewed last night, while I overslept
(Groping for comfort in the net of my dream
About the nearing end of days). So, I chew the pill,
Readying up for my 4 o'clock early
With the rottweiler who beams back at me
From the wet, black mouth of my boiler room.

CATE CARLOW

is an MA student of archaeology at the
University of Durham. She has previously
been published in the *Christopher Tower Poetry
Competition*, *The Times* and student journals.

NIGHTMARE SONNET

When it is midnight and another murdered day
has broken its back on the bleak midwinter of my life;
when wasps go anticlimatically without stitching
their stings onto the sarsaparilla clench of my fist;
when each day is a year, and each year is a fiscal policy
poaching poor wallets for secluded offshore accounts;
when every failed interaction is stuffed achromatically
into my penguin processions to the ends of the office;
when I can no longer switch on in the mornings without
charging my bones through a mechanical coffee;
when there is no hope beyond hoping that someday soon
hope itself will give everything up as a bad job;
then I will know my life's allotted hours are done
and the world at large has already moved on.

MARK CHAMBERLAIN
has been published in *Magma,
The Hudson Review, Finished Creatures, The
Financial Times*, and *FAKE by Corrupted Poetry*.
His poetry criticism has been published in *The
Times Literary Supplement*.

THE BEST NEW BRITISH AND IRISH POETS 2019-2021

IDEAS

My tongue turned into
the head of a goat
   its eyes meeting mine
   from my mouth in the mirror
   as I went to brush my teeth

having been woken by my neighbours
politicking on the street

   It said *imagine*
   what they will say what
   they will do when they

   see me here inside you

   Its ears scratched my
   hard palate

   where I used to raise
the body of my tongue

to make the sound *y* in
you yearn yellow

   I wanted to call it
Young Eye – its pupils
   wide-cut windows on
   a blood-borne art –

but knew I
couldn't

so I called it Architect – its nose
       tapping the bump
       behind my teeth for the Ts –

       and I opened the window so the stench
of the long vowel   *Aaaa*
sunk down to the street

REGI CLAIRE

grew up in Switzerland, and
lives in Edinburgh with her husband and
their golden retriever, where she is a teaching
fellow at Edinburgh University. Her first-ever
poem won the Mslexia/PBS Women's Poetry
Competition 2019, and was shortlisted for the
Forward Prize for Best Single Poem 2020. She
is the winner of a UBS Cultural Foundation
award, and a two-time finalist for the Saltire
Scottish Book of the Year awards. Claire is a
former Royal Literary Fund Fellow and RLF
Lector for Reading Round Scotland, and is the
author of two novels and two story collections.
www.regiclaire.com

THE LAST WOMAN ON EARTH

After the rains you stand in a lane fringed with
Queen Anne's lace and hollyhock
in this cold northern city
in the eucalyptus zing of a tree that reaches for the sky
and flays its skin in perpetual renewal.

How have you come to be here?
You don't know. You woke to the trill of a bird
and there you were, the last woman on earth, hair and face
dripping, clothes sodden, even the socks inside
your boots. Even the note in your pocket.

What note?
Something, a scrap of paper. An advert for pills. A torn circular from
the IFAW – you can almost make out an image.
Maybe part of a letter, handwritten, typed, printed, yet always
illegible. Beside the hedge are more

scraps, much smaller, wetter, clinging like fake flowers to the
          knee-high grasses.

Urging you to step across, strip those stems bare,
ransack the verge. Urging you to go and
piece them back together,
paste them if necessary. Or force them into a ball,
squeeze them in your palm

into a papier-mâché bullet that
needs no gun,
only a softness to strike
home.

CHARLOTTE CORNELL

is from Kent, England, where she is a mum to three young children. After time spent writing speeches for politicians, she now "enjoys writing fiction and creativity in a different way". Much of her poetry is inspired by the Thames Estuary and the sights, sounds and history of the South East of England. Charlotte won the Canterbury Poet of the Year in 2020.

THE GIFT OF MRS ANN THWAYTES, 1839

Ann Thwaytes was a leading Victorian philanthropist. Among the buildings she funded are many schools, surgeries, chapels and the Herne Bay Clock Tower.

I

I was never good wi' words. Too many syllables and my tongue trip'd, coiling back to choke consonants that might ha' thought to be second spoils. Thoughts would lodge there like fat cud in a heifer's gullet an' teacher would say there were a place for weak witterins wi' no gifts like me. Despite my reading, it weren't behind a desk, he said.

II

To not be wed at thirty-one sent Ma away for good. She said I were wickin' all the life from her. The old college kept her in the end, as she couldn't pay. I bore her shame like them slaps husbands gi' wives for servants to see. Poverty the ribbon tied tight across my jowl. I kept thinkin' that perhaps a blue coat might wear me awhile, but that didn't suit, so I look'd broader.

III

When Ma died, I did say yes, but I could still smell my sister on his skin. He muzzled tha' I was his true Queen Anne, but I preferred ancients to kings, so told him to drop the e. I liked it plain, I said. No need to wrap up convenience. Yet before more important men could tally the cost of any weak fire I might ha' lit in him, my Crassus was dead.

IV

My coin must be sticky for so many to come buzzing now. I ha' been quite feted and favoured. Each gift I build taller than t'last, laying each foundation with my hand manly spread. I build proudly tall, thinkin' one day some cane-whipped girl or bride-to-be will pass sayin', 'look, she stands just as well as he' and change her path.

SIMON COSTELLO

is an Irish poet. His poetry has been
published and is forthcoming in *The Stinging Fly,
The Rialto, Magma, The Irish Times, Poetry Ireland
Review*, amongst others. In 2021 he was awarded
first prize in The Rialto Nature and Place Poetry
Competition and was a recipient of a Literature
Bursary Award from the Arts Council of
Ireland.

COCOON

You orbit your own sun,
butting your head against
the hot bulb of my kitchen.
You might smash the glass,
light pouring out for you
to swallow whole. But
there is method. You need
a fixed point to guide you
over fern & earth, right?
When a city of insects rises
& makes for the open door
I've left, they'll find you,
behind the cupboard,
lacquered in dust, slapped
by the pale moon-white
of my palm, the fire you tasted
long gone, by then
you'll be someone else entirely

EVAN COSTIGAN

lives on the West coast of Ireland,
and holds an MPhil in Writing from the
University of South Wales. His poetry has
appeared in *Poetry Ireland Review, The North,
The Stinging Fly, The Irish Times, The Moth,
The Stony Thursday Book, Cyphers, The Best
New British and Irish Poets 2018*, amongst others.
He is a past winner of the Boyle Arts Festival
Poetry Competition, and the Francis Ledwidge
International Poetry Award. In 2017, Costigan
won both the Red Line Book Festival Poetry
Competition, and the Oliver Goldsmith Literary
Festival Poetry Competition; he was shortlisted
for a Hennessy Literary Award in 2014.
www.evancostigan.com

THE KISS

Burning down to the stub of my last cigarette
with the sun a dipping disc behind an office block,
I was thinking of a girl last week, figuring a next move,

when, from opposite sides of Parque Metropolitano,
the couple closed on each other with the urgency
of a parent reunited with a missing child.

I watched her eyelids crinkle as the space
between their lips diminished, on touch
her shoulders slackening in his arms

as if he'd loosened something in her,
all the while his face crept with the branching shadows
of some great tree, except he knew

none of this, since he too, was in a rapture –
her fingers disappearing through his hair.
The sun bathed them in light

for just that moment, and as they shrank,
entwined, into the distance, something
was unpacking in me. I realised then

that couple would cost me – that I would be years
ghosting in and out of lives across countries
without striking their seam of gold.

A.M. COUSINS

lives in Wexford Town in Ireland.
Her poems can be found in various journals
including *Poetry Ireland Review, The Stinging
Fly* and online in *poethead.wordpress.com*. She
also writes memoir and local history essays for
'Sunday Miscellany' on RTE Radio 1. Her first
collection of poetry, REDRESS, was published
in 2021 (Revival Press).

EASTER SATURDAY 2013

after Paul Perry

There's something indecent about Meyler's counter:
cadavers harvested – sole brothers, tender bellies slit open
and exposed – Lenten fare, slaughtered for us.
There is so much love in the heart of a seal so

point your finger at John Dory, tell him
you know him, you know who bruised his skin,
who leaned over the side of a canoe on a hot day in Galilee
and marked him with the print of His thumb.

The Quay lads hid penicillin in a fish and made a blind seal see
selkie girls leave their beds, peel off their pelts,
shin over the sea-wall and flippetty flop up the hill.
Their whiskers brush the window of Kehoe's Pub and Parlour

and they blink pale lashes as a girl dances with a scarf
for the fishermen and boys who drove like maniacs
up the pier when the summons came, because all they have
is the ebb and flow – the shimmy – of her poetic *ars*.

Across the chapel-yard· the Exsultet – the greatest story
ever told – the sea cleaves in two, Egyptians are smited.
A bowl of fire warms the paschal sanctuary as incense smokes
and gladdens. Can you believe this? Then the Chans are baptised –

the four old souls from the Takeaway in Selskar
anointed with chrism, heads bent and washed, waves
of applause for the new brethren. The handsome priest,
under unbearable duress, lifts high the cross, shivers and waits.

ELENA CROITORU

is a Pushcart Prize nominee, and holds
an MSt in Creative Writing from the University
of Cambridge. She reached second place in the
Bart Wolffe Poetry Prize, and third place in
the Open House poetry competition. She was
shortlisted for the Alpine Fellowship, Wasafiri
New Writing Prize, Gregory O'Donoghue
Prize, Emerging Writer Award 2018, amongst
other prizes. Croitoru's work has been published
in *Litro, Southword,* and elsewhere.

THE ROAD TO SCHOOL NO. 10

By then, our churches had been rebuilt
but God did not return.
The older communists retreated
into their flats and I would walk
under their balconies,
along fossilised pavements,
on my way to school no. 10.

Sometimes I would see a man,
naked from the waist up
or down, I can't remember.
He would macerate his arms
in liquor, then he would wave
and I would wonder
if my homework was good enough
to get me out.

Sometimes I would break
into the stadium which took
the loneliness out of our town,
and encircled it with wooden benches.
Its silence made me think
about the places we called home.

Sometimes I would run
into the girl who told me
not to laugh, before she showed me
her two missing knuckles.
I nodded because I knew
how that felt. Those bones were
the first things she noticed about me.

Sometimes I grew, not up but sideways,
building a new century city in my mind,
shedding the concrete skins of tower blocks,
putting up one glass panel after another,
so we could all see
what our country had done to our people.

KELLY DAVIS

was born in London, and now lives in
Maryport, on the West Cumbrian coast, where
she works from home as a freelance editor. She
studied at Oxford and worked in publishing in
Australia and the UK in the 1980s. Davis's poems
have been published in magazines, including
Mslexia, *The Journal* and *Southlight,* along with
many anthologies. She won a *Magma* subscribers'
competition in 2018 and was commended by
Helen Mort in the 2020 Borderlines Poetry
Competition. In 2020 she was also shortlisted
for the international Aesthetica Creative
Writing Award for Poetry. 'Floating'
first appeared in *Shooter Literary Magazine*,
Issue 12 (Animal Love), Winter 2021.

FLOATING

While swimming, I noticed
a dark speck floating in the pool.
A wasp, I thought. *Probably dead.*
Not wanting to risk a sting
I cupped my hands below, and
whooshed water and insect aside.

Beached on the tiles,
the wasp heaved rhythmically.
A shipwrecked sailor
flung ashore,
gasping, seeping
chlorinated water.

One umbrella-spoke leg
repeatedly tried to unfurl,
a limp wing attempted to open.
Two little movements that
sent it spinning: a one-oared boat
paddling nowhere.

Using a leaf as a scoop,
I gently placed it on dry tiles,
then swam a few more lengths
and returned – to find it
still at last.

EMMA MAHON DECKER

is an Irish-American journalist,
currently based in Oregon. She grew
up in County Galway and the
Pacific Northwest.

TAKE ME HOME, TIERNASCRAGH

you would think counting sheep to fall asleep would be the thing to do
in a place like this
surrounded by them and their calls
but I always counted cars
the few that took our small country road at night
how many of their shadows shape-shifted across my bedroom walls
curving their way around my body
just like the ancient, winding road they traveled on

I counted how many sweets I could get with my euros
and the number of shells we brought back from the sea
how many candles should we light at the church today?
one for you, one for the dog, one for me

but I never counted the steps to the graveyard
how many it took to carry my grandfather there
or the number of fish I caught in the Shannon
at the bend where we watched the final snips of his hair
swirl away in the eddies

because some numerals mark moments
some are habit

and some are just the sounds of footsteps on gravel
and the doves in the trees
counting down to nothing
one sheep, two sheep, three

CLIVE DONOVAN

currently resides in Devon, UK, where he is a full-time poet. His work has been published in a variety of magazines, including *The Journal, Agenda, Acumen, Poetry Salzburg Review, Pennine Platform, Prole, Stand* and *The Transnational*.

THE ROSES OF HELIOGABALUS

(And the paradox of *damnatio memoriae*)

They hang by the ceiling, soft and limp;
Cartloads of roses, threshed from the tyrant's fields.
Their dense weight settled, they breathe on the feast.

Their celestial scent pervades the air,
Mingled with earthy smells of dormice stuffed
In the kitchen with pork-paste and pine nuts;

Boiled ostrich, flamingos and parrots,
Musky sweat of oiled dwarf wrestlers,
Delicate perfumes of luxury dancing girls…

As they work through the menu to dessert – the *secundae*,
The emperor, Heliogabalus, gives a great belch
And on a wave of his big royal hand, the roof-gates collapse

Expelling their ambush of costly surprise:
And as the chosen ones inhale with their choked-off sighs,
Petals, light as the breath they put a stop to,

Mixed with spilt wine and trampled dates and honey cakes,
Do they recognise, these guests, they are the top-billed wonder
Stars of this night's scandalous, unforgotten cabaret?

EGE DÜNDAR

is a 26-year-old writer and activist
from Turkey. Exiled to the UK due to political
pressures in his home country, Dündar currently
resides in Berlin. He co-authored a fable
book, produced and presented a weekly music
program on NumberOne TV and worked as a
Sunday columnist in *Milliyet Daily* newspaper.
His writing has been published in outlets such
as *BirGün, LeManyak, Cumhuriyet Daily, An-
Nahar* and *PEN Transmissions*. A graduate
of International Politics at City University
London, Dündar currently works at PEN
International. He is the founder and coordinator
of the young writers network *İlkyaz and Creative
Witnesses*, the solidarity action series bringing
together musicians and creative artists in support
of writers at risk.

STIFF LIKE TREES, WE GROW OLDER

Once supple as toddlers, like the pea green stem,
We were thick as thieves with our few leaves,
Once, long before countless shed in the breeze.

Once humble hunchbacks, we curved for the light
Our senses rooted in, delved out of sight.
We formed bulky, crusted barks,
In seared layers over our warm blood,
And tirelessly swayed in its ebb and tides,
As the bones calcified.

Shrouded like trees we grew older,
Heavy on the shoulders, no more the receptive shape
No more the eager reach.
Meanderings subsided at optimal heights.
We would've been fine without speech, finer perhaps
Like the trees,
Anchored further in a bit of our earth, every season, stretching the skin,
Needing only but a cup of water to grow within,
Finding novelty even in the wind, creation in drifting pollen.

I remember the sky was closer, before I got taller,
When like a sprouts spike through the earthly seed
I first looked up,
Life never before nor again to feel so palpable,
Like a baby or a tree at birth,
From the tried and the true,

Moulded in mud, dreaming of the blue.

PATRICK JAMES ERRINGTON

currently resides in Edinburgh, and is the author of *Glean* and *Field Studies*. He is the French translator of P.J. Harvey's poetry collection *The Hollow of the Hand*, and his poems appear in *The Iowa Review, Oxford Poetry, Boston Review, The Cincinnati Review* and elsewhere. Errington has won or been highly commended for prizes such as *The London Magazine* Poetry Competition and The National Poetry Competition.

BURNING THE FIELDS

Had I lain longer in the firebreak
of the senses. Had colour lingered,

patient, in the skin – already, the end
breeds beneath the bed, needles

out from the dark, veining the sheets
with a thin skein of frost. What animal

haunts the spelt, shivers
the broken stalks? Somewhere a lancet

of geese slits my chest like a skyline
bleeding winter.   Had I frayed

my teeth apart, made a nest in the down
of my mouth, would you have stayed?

ELIO ESCOFFERY

is a British, Jamaican poet born in London. After attaining his Bachelors degree in Photography and an MA in Art History, he moved to Copenhagen, Denmark, where he is currently residing. At the age of 17, Elio began writing poetry while trying to process his father's illness. Race, love and decay are prominent topics within his work. Escoffery is working on his debut novel.

WHEN IT WAS

She postured a flower to me
With our mouths wet,
and the white sky receding,
this object cut all stillness
Yellow winged, copper red centred,
peacefully sat upon its breathing stem
Pausing, she looked bright somewhere,
distracted by soft blushes
By now I faced the wind's teeth
We caught the air, landing backwards

D.W. EVANS

was born in Newcastle-upon-Tyne,
and now lives on the Island of Jersey. His
poems won the Alan Jones Memorial Prize in
2019 and 2020, received a highly commended
award from the Acumen Poetry Competition
and was shortlisted for Ó Bhéal's 7th Five
Words International Poetry Competition 2020,
along with being shortlisted for Ó Bhéal's
2021 competition. His poems have appeared in
the *Frogmore Papers* and *Proverse Mingled Voices*.
'Rapunzel' first appeared in the April 2020
edition of *The A3 Review*.

RAPUNZEL

Hospital chic was never your style.
The surgical shift, listeria blue,
colour, cut, gingham check –
contorting like migraine
against gangrene curtains.

They'd washed your hair.
Fanning over a white pillow,
flat, lank, all life combed out.
Something
I never knew
until we finally met
in that tented lair:

                the length of it.

Hidden, no suggestion
beneath steely smells – setting lotion, hairspray air,
grips, headscarves, rollers, penning, teasing

                                      all

that hair.
Was it always there?

You were never at the seaside.
            No.

In the gallery of memory, small you,
gold framed, the hospital finale,

                you, your secret hair:
silver with a spot of uncertain medical purple.

The image should fade – polaroids do –

or be swapped: you, beach, laughing,
waving a cigarette, the dog mid-air,
carefree in Whitley Bay.

Still, your fingernails are neat,
near perfection against the pallid sheet.
You would have approved of that.

ROSEANNE FAHEY

is a 21-year-old student living in Offaly,
Ireland, studying Creative Writing at the
National University of Ireland, Galway. Her
poetry and prose have been published in *In
Parenthesis*, *Dead Fern Press*, and *ROPES*,
amongst others.

HOME

I am from antiques.
From broken bookcases to dressers with no handles.
I am from the two-storey on the street
with two front steps, a rustic gate, a house that's always cold.
I am bluebells,
beloved by my mother, although I am allergic.
I am from cousins on Christmas Eve and barely reaching
five feet tall.
From Pauline and Pat, though it's just Pat now.
I am from spouses, who choose to stay in
different rooms, different houses,
different countries, different continents.
From "stop feeling sorry for yourself" and "you're my favourite child".
From weekly morning Mass until mum got cancer,
and hospital wards with bars on the windows.
I am from Tullamore and Cahersiveen,
chicken goujons and chicken curry,
and my sister saying the only thing she knows about me
is that I'm obsessed with chicken.
Pink lipstick on my mother's corpse.
My sister's face in six photo frames, and my face in one.
I am from furniture that I didn't choose,
and the family that said
they wished one of us had died instead.

REBECCA FAULKNER

is a London-born children's rights advocate, climate activist and poet. She currently lives in Brooklyn, New York. Her poetry has been published or is forthcoming in *Smoke Magazine, The Maine Review, On the Seawall, Ink Sweat & Tears, Into the Void* and Passengers Press.

PERMIT ME TO WRITE MY OWN ENDING

I will tell you a secret as you burn through your journey,
thirsty & thankless: I used to watch you in the mirror
plotting conquests in your Levis, your shirt unbuttoned

for the revolution. Airmail envelopes buried in drawers,
a maze of years collapsing with each infidelity, your reflection
ordering me to trust you. But I am tired of your real skin,

of history & its thickening red voice. Ink on your fingers
& girls in your crosshairs, I taste abandon in the bite
of your cologne. Now it is spring – permit me

to write my own ending. Tonight I will slip out the back,
no longer witness to your misadventures, their gap teeth
& low-cut blouses & you, stray dog, your drooling jaws

open wide, reaching into your new decade. I have closed
myself before, a kitchen in midwinter. But I refuse to wait
with the cat that sits on the balcony, urging me to leave.
You will find ash where I burned your clothes.

MADISON FEARN

is a recent university graduate residing in
Sheffield, South Yorkshire, where she currently
works as a supply teacher. Fearn's work has
been published in *Acumen*.

THE CREATURES IN THE FOG

This image forged in marble:
Two beasts with necks of sturdy trunk,
knees cocked like smoking guns.

The Earth inverted.
Stamps of foreign mail
that punctuate the grass
in half-moon crescents.

They do not recognise this terrain
under the muzzle of the fog.
I wonder what they say to one another
when their snorts pierce through the veil.

This moment paraglides,
and I cannot think of a time
when there were not two creatures

in the mist. I wonder
who needed to see their shadows straddled together?
For it cannot have been me.

REBECCA RIVER FORBES

is a British-Mauritian. She writes poems, short
stories and performing stand up-comedy. Her
short stories have been nominated for a Pushcart
Prize, longlisted for Fiction Factory's Short
Story Prize and shortlisted for the Exeter Short
Story Prize. Her poetry has been published in
The Elevation Review, *River River*, *West Trade
Review*, and *Route 7 Review,* amongst others.
Twitter @bohobo101

WHITE WORDS

Not old enough to fluently run,
But transported across continents,
To a stark place where the cold chewed on my bones.
They gave me shame to flay my own skin.
No one spoke my language in this cold place.
Vile words lay under their tongues,
Words that I refused the bitter taste of.
Refuge in armoured silence against this nowhere land.
It was not temporary.
I drown over and over in aching for something,
But the memories become memories of stories,
Instead of the faces and the scents,
And the feeling on my skin of warmth from bodies and the sun.
No one came for me; those ties have strained and snapped.
And now I was stranded out of reach.
I learned how to shape their words into weapons.
Because my own words had left me too,
I took theirs instead—a meticulous thief.
So I could cut them deeply, and they would never forget.
Pulled from the futile grip of a child.
A piece that was taken away before I knew what it was,
But I always wondered what should be in that sick space.

TANATSEI GAMBURA

is a poet and cultural practitioner.
She is the author of *Things I Have Forgotten
Before*, her debut pamphlet (Bad Betty Press).
Her work explores the possibilities of re-
memory and healing in the aftermath of
individual, familial, national and collective
trauma. Tanatsei is the runner-up to the
inaugural Amsterdam Open Book Prize (2020),
a Rebecca Swift Foundation Women Poets' Prize
longlistee (2020), and a recipient of the Library
Of Africa and The African Diaspora (LOATAD)
and Savannah Center for Contemporary Art
(SCCA) Writing Residency (2021). Poems of
hers appear in *Prufrock Magazine, The London
Reader, New Coin Poetry Journal*, and *Poetry
London,* amongst others. She is an alumnus of
the British Council residency, 'These Images
are Stories', the inaugural Obsidian Foundation
Writer's Retreat, and the Writerz & Scribez
Griot's Well residency.

CAUSE OF DEATH

We do not
discuss politics
at the dining table.
We might stab
it with a fork,
lift it to a trembling
mouth and swallow.
We nudge it
to the edge
of our plates,
look past it,
scrub them with
barbed wire,
slit our hands,
drain our blood
in the sink.
These hunger strikes
are a shovel in a graveyard.
Citizen is the tombstone.
Cause of death is silence;
Cause of death is a scream.
Somewhere between them
my country buried me.

MICHAEL GLENFIELD

is an emerging Irish poet, and MA
graduate of Creative Writing from Royal
Holloway University of London. He is currently
a PhD candidate at the University of Bristol,
where he resides and teaches.

ENCHANTED

Many old gods ascend from their graves; they are disenchanted
and hence take the form of impersonal forces

— Max Weber, *Science as a Vocation*

In the last great illusion of our age
we have been charmed into believing
that big data enlarges our lives,
and in this theology of statistics
supplicants kneel before almighty
algorithms which watch them from birth,
and if only we could see the cell walls
which enclose the human datum we might
escape the upward crawl that follows us
from childhood in the fallacy of ever-
increasing linear progress through tests
which begin at six in attempts to prove
that no child has been left behind in the race
to divide learning into increments
of escalating digits, as our youth
are sent to market fit only for a job
watching spreadsheets with all the intent
of a sniper or curator of fine art
while numbers are made to perform miracles
in the war against profit margins
or seed banks or illiteracy
as our elders and betters create towers
of data in cheerless acronyms
crafting inaccessible masterpieces
of inarticulate fiction which show
how yield is up, down or choking double
helixes into what we laughingly call
the system where complaints are useless,
apostates ignored, for numbers cannot

be blamed for our overconfidence
in their abilities which is as inbuilt
as their inability to express
anything as simple as a narrative
or the truth or the abstract way people
often smile as they walk alone through this
great enchanted garden we call breathing.

RICH GOODSON

teaches English to refugee and migrant
teenagers in Nottingham, where he is currently
training to be a counsellor. His debut pamphlet,
Mr Universe, was chosen as a Poetry Book Society
Pamphlet Choice in 2017 and his work has
appeared in anthologies that include *In Transit:
Poems of Travel* and *The Poetry of Sex*.

WHELK

My grandmother's ear's a broken sea-smoothed whelk.
I hook two fingers into it, ease it from the suck
of the side of her sallow head
& hold it up for the both of us to see.
Ninety-five years of sand shush out of it
into the swirling-mauve bladderwrack of the nursing home carpet.

Is that mine? she says. Put it to your ear! Tell me if you hear Skegness!

So I put it to my ear & yesssssssssssssssssssssssssssssssssssss: Skegness!
of which in her womanhood she bore the salty weight five times
& pretended to like it.

Then I press its exoskeleton hard against my ear until
out of the waves' white noise
comes the voice she had for her daughter, my mother, in 1969:

I'll not abide no harlot, not under my roof. I'll not abide it.
You pray it don't take, girl. Get down on your knees & pray it don't take.
But if it do – God forbid – you flush it – we flush it –
through your you-know your down-there.
& it'll be as good as buggered & gone in the water
& folk'll be none the wiser.

I fit the whelk & all that good advice
back – with a squelch – into the side of her head
just as the January sun keens through the extravagant loudhailer
of the amaryllis (*Scarlet Clown*) I've bought her.
The world shifts.
& Małgorzata rattles in the four o' clock trolley
with tea, & two Jammy Dodgers
& is showing us how nails become miracles at the Hollywood Nail Bar.

My grandmother beams. *This is my grandson who went to Oxford!*

Ah, so I'm to be married off
but the tide's already rising
already slopping around our calves & icy cold!

Blast your eyes, we'll none of us go gently!

Małgorzata swims out of the room for help.
A hundred toffee-wrappers float out after her, like a halo of dead wasps.
Suddenly there's only a foot of shuddering air between the water & the ceiling.
My grandmother paws for my ear & whispers:

She'll make a good cuppa, but watch 'er, lad, watch 'er.
They're all the same.
Slatterns.
& strangers to a hoover.

MAZ HEDGEHOG

is a writer and performer, currently
residing in Manchester. She has previously
worked with Penguin, Blue Peter and
performed at events across the UK.
@MazHedgehog

BELLS

Touch me
Tap muffled rib
Ring padded sternum with
Hands unlike copper
Hands unlike tin
Unwrap cloth against whisper
Press hands unlike vespers
Ring
  Clemens
     Pia
       Dulcis

Etch peccator into my nape
Clap hand over mouth
Listen: bells like winter
So full of empty
So yearning
So hunger and revulsion
So touch me
Not to pull and play noon time
Nor forge bells for the steeple
Nor etch sensuum into my shoulder
Into my crown
Into my wishes
    Still copper/tin
    Still molten/pliable
I forged more copper than tin
Etched blank
Pressed smooth
Mouth closed
    Incomplete
Touch me
Open lips like vespers

Print miserere
Print woman
Clap hands over lies
Say

              woman is a bell
Less copper than tin
Forge me less copper than tin
      Touch me
Christening
        Touch me
Death knell
           Touch me
Whole and ringing

DAVID HEIDENSTAM

grew up in England. Trained as a political
scientist, he has worked at jobs ranging from
editor to sailboat-delivery cook/crewman. In
the 1970s he was one of those responsible for
the *Body* books series (*Man's Body, Woman's
Body, Child's Body*). His poems have appeared
in *Agenda, Ambit,* and *The American Journal of
Poetry*, along with anthologies published by
Faber & Faber and Carcanet. He is the author
of *Tales for my Dog: 80 microfictions from humour to
horror* and the stage play *In the Beginning…* 'Other
Eden' first appeared in *Ambit.*

OTHER EDEN

The birds fly backwards. From the trees
The glow of blossoms lights the dusk.
The moon's an absence in a silver sky.
Not it, but earth, is made of cheese.
Loved and unloved together lie.
The lions are vegetarian.
Bus conductors are never brusque.
The young revere librarians.
In winter only fridges freeze,
And all art's proletarian.

MAEVE HENRY

currently resides in Oxford, and holds an MA in Creative Writing from Oxford Brookes. She was shortlisted for the Wasafiri New Writing Prize in 2018, and the inaugural Brotherton Prize in 2019. Her poetry has been published in *Live Canon, Mslexia, Magma*, and elsewhere.

www.maevehenry.com

FROM THE WEBSITE OF THE NATIONAL MUSEUM OF IRAQ

(i) Harp

Buried with its harpist, whose finger bones curve
over the space of vanished strings, the Harp of Ur.
A glory of gold, silver, shell and lapis lazuli,
nothing is known of its musician, found
in a human pyramid of girls murdered
by blunt force to the head, and re-arranged
after death to lie peacefully in each other's laps
around the central figure of their queen.
More is understood about the fate
of the Harp, looted from the museum,
broken to pieces in a car park, its sacred
bull head drowning in a flooded bank vault.

(ii) Tablets

Perhaps this was Eresh, this cluster of low hills
on the flat plain, next to nowhere.
Layers of mud brick dwellings generations deep,
abandoned when the Euphrates changed
its course. Robbers cut into the mounds, but left
the herringbone brickwork and sunken basins,
the fire pits, damp courses, and the clay tablets. Dug
from beneath the scorched end wall, along with bitumen,
potsherds, burnt matting and fish bones, is sacred wisdom;
also lists of names and occupations –
lost over again in looted Baghdad, when the museum fell.

(iii) Gertrude Bell's Letter

Baghdad, July the Second.

Darling Father,
Today, a practice by the Royal Air Force.
A quarter of a mile from where we sat
on Diala dyke, they dropped two heavy bombs
from three thousand feet, a village set alight.
Later I went swimming with Major Gore.
A blazing afternoon. You cannot think
how fine it is to drop into the cool
swift river! He agrees no other Arabs
have the chance we offer these. And yet I wonder
are they men enough to take it? Please send me
news of Herbert, and dearest Elsa.
Ever, my dear, your very affectionate daughter.

JOHANNA HIGGINS

is a Criminal Lawyer, and an elected member of
the Royal Historical Society. Higgins currently
lives on the North West coast of Ireland, and
in addition to writing poetry has a particular
interest in 16th Century England.

THUSIA

My friends advise me in several ways
On where to put my Love.
Each one long dead and
Red earth heaped upon his beautiful head.

Ludovicus says I can grasp the arrow of this pain
And sear it through my heart for Him.
Which I do
Each time I think of you.

Frederic only makes it worse,
But in such a sweet way.
With him I sway to endless chords of sound
And shield my longing.

A priest and poet soothes and calms my fear,
And knows each beat of human heart,
And tells me that eternity is near.
And how each swallowing of life
Is always the beginning of everything.

And a martyr says
In heaven it shall be lawful to
Love and be loved as we desire.
My heart then leaps and longs and lies
Down before this tide.
And I offer it up.
A sacrifice of yearning.

DANIEL HINDS

lives in Newcastle, England, and holds a
Distinction in his English Literature MA, for which he
won two prestigious scholarships. Hinds won the Poetry
Society's Timothy Corsellis Young Critics Prize 2018
and his prose poem review of Jay Bernard's *Surge* was
a winner of the Shortlist Book Review Competition
2020. He was shortlisted for the Streetcake Experimental
Writing Prize 2019, the Terry Kelly Poetry Prize 2018
and his poems have been highly commended in the
Newcastle Centre for the Literary Arts Water Poetry
Competition. His poetry has been published or is
forthcoming in *The London Magazine, The New European,
Amethyst Review, The Honest Ulsterman*, amongst
others. An essay was published in *Pre-Raphaelite
Society Review*. Twitter: @DanielGHinds

THE PACT OF WATER

A bargain was struck
Like the wet smiting of a storm upon a shore.

They signed in a squirt of squid ink spray.
Our pen tip crossed the white threshold.

We looked up to them, those gods in cockle
And sea bone suits, shining upon the crest
Of a tsunami wave of Atlantean awe.

We hockled our liquid libation in their drink
And the slick grease of our phlegm spread.

Put your ear to a stone shell or a seal's black flank,
Hear the submerged voices raised in the world's blood.

Now we look down in meropian blindness,
Discern no cities capped beneath blue braes.

We let the water fall through our hands.
It leaves a tentacle pucker mark.

NYLE HOLIHAN

currently lives in Yorkshire, and is a professional folk musician, specialising in frailing banjo and Appalachian folklore. He holds an MA in Creative Writing from the University of Kent, and has presented his poetry at Folkestone SALT festival, The Ash Archive, The Norfolk & Norwich festival and Broadstairs Folk Week.

KUDZU

I dreamt
leant against the backbar
of a shore lapped
by a water glass-clear
                  and sharp salted

not quite remembered
and held fast by a fraying pocket

empty
caught against a stray nail
the thickening smell of curing leather
    cadence of turmeric and cumin

murmur of voices
a mumbling dispute
     quantities and prices
grain and livestock
a mindless space
between wet-eyed barflies

I feel my skin dry
     things slow
my empty stare
catching a pupil
             that stretches as it moves
I see now
the long flat pupil of a sheep

a voice in bleats
near human
  the grey mottled ram

127

      bows its head

patient
as my great-grandmother
my father's mother's mother
pulls maggots from its wounded leg
murmuring

     a long wordless reassurance
deft with the short sharp knife
    its cutting edge
          flashes

while the rest is dulled
        grey with old blood
olive wood burns
    with a bitter reek
the men crowd a low table

the sun slides white
until the very last moments

    then grows vast

the cardamom scent
    of tea glasses
drifts up with the light
heavy brows
and a nose like my own
      silhouetted against the pink
and orange

so then
great-grandparents
      old already
in a slow walk arm in arm
to a hillside chapel

rich in smoke and gilt
    saints' faces
    flat and fearful
thumb on their third fingers
     turned in shame

    from the bottom left of the fresco
    wincing souls
       gripping one another
caught in a deep red river
the long fleshy tongue
emanating
         from a muscular hellmouth

with great patience
she lights a slim beeswax candle
         then another

a beer bottle rattles
    slammed impatiently down
      I un-lid another
    a sheep's eye
    flashes no gratitude

my grandmother's first husband
sailed first to these ports
where the water shivers
in the colour of old steel

he lived many short lives
as they trudged west
slipping away from ceremony
falling saints' names
      stains on dry earth

PATRICK HOLLOWAY

is an Irish writer of fiction and poetry.
He won second place in the Raymond
Carver Fiction Contest and has previously been
shortlisted for numerous awards including the
Dermot Healy Poetry Prize, The Over The
Edge New Writer of the Year Award and Bath
Short Story Award. Holloway's work has been
published by *Poetry Ireland Review, The Irish
Times, Overland Literary Journal, Write Bloody
Publishing, New Voices Scotland, The Stinging Fly*,
and elsewhere. His short story 'Counting Stairs'
was highly commended for the Manchester
Fiction Prize, and his story *The Lift and the Fox
and the Lilies* was selected for the Hennessy
New Irish Writing in 2019.

TO THAT OTHER ME BEHIND THE LOOKING GLASS

Go! To that backstreet & graffiti something obscene,
To Machu Picchu, to Milan. Go obsolete. Go back to your
Teens & piss in the teachers' toilets. Make a scene. Wear a top hat
In the afternoon & spend days thumbing old photographs.
Go sideways, upways, timeways to your birth. Sift through clouds
To find your worth. Go to your father's grave & leave nothing
On the earth. Go far. Go further. Go brave.
Go to sea & wave at the moon, beyond the finish line & start again.
Go to womb. To a home that never existed. Back to the farmer's warehouse
& burn it down to ashes. Go alone. Go on. Go to your bedroom
& lay on the floor, eyes to the stars, to the unknown.

Be! That silver painted boy juggling traffic cones. That black man with a swag
& cigar. That father who knows how to balance the world on his shoulders.
Be ash. Be bones. Your mother at the hob, burnt arms,
Humming & cooking. Be a country, be an island, be a lost boy in Neverland,
Always looking for you. Be Hook. Be lippy & leggy & ready to fuck (& be fucked);
Be the fuck up, the fuck over. Be a candle, a pullover, the main course
& leftovers. Foam. Be a mountain dressed in white. Be an X chromosome,
Be the fight & the fought & the fought over. Be thought.
Be older, wrinkled & veiny & eyeing up death with a smirk.
Be nothing more than breath.

Live! With death in your pocket, with Jupiter in your eye. Live with that tattooed
Boy your parents disapprove of. Live on the streets asking why; live without
Asking, live without withouts. Live on music & dancing & beats in your feet.
Live long. Live reading & writing & forgetting it all; live like a song, off-key,
Live like synchronisation, with fascination at all that is unknown & free. Live
With her, & him, & him & him & her. Live with a middle finger to the sky.
Live poor & poorer until you're rich with living; live inside your skin, inside your
Fur; outside your life & soul; live within. With your heart in your hands,
Pumping & bleeding & ready to throw, live it all, what you've done &
Haven't & know & unknow. Live today. Live tomorrow. See how it goes.

TAMSIN HOPKINS

currently resides in London. A winner
of the Aesthetica Creative Writing Prize, her
poems have appeared in *The New Statesman*,
Tears in the Fence, and *The Interpreter's House*,
amongst others. Her published pamphlet is
titled *Inside the Smile*.

DIRECTIONS

Nine Plays in Seven Acts

I

To combat the increasing callousness of mankind,
J Peachum, a man of business, has opened a shop
where the poorest of the poor can acquire an exterior that will touch
the hardest of hearts

Through the partitioning wall at the right we hear a prosecutor's voice
Swathed in white sheets, a shroud covers the face

A small, tumble-down chapel long abandoned
Dark poplar trees loom on one side
Beyond them the cherry orchard begins

The sky that shows around the dime white building is a peculiarly
tender blue-almost
turquoise, which gracefully attenuates the atmosphere of decay, you
can almost feel the warm breath of the brown river

II

A warm day in early August 1936, outside the village of Ballybeg,
County Donegal

There is a sycamore tree off right. One of its branches reaches over
part of the house.

Upstage centre is a garden seat. The (unseen) boy has been making
two kites and pieces of wood,

Paper, cord etc are lying on the ground close to the
garden seat. One kite is almost complete

III

1 Enter Roderigo and Iago

2 Enter Montano, Governor of Cyprus,

3 Enter Cassio with two others

4 Enter Iago and Othello

5(2) Enter Othello with a light, and Desdemona in her bed asleep

IV

The Poker Night:
The kitchen suggests that sort of lurid nocturnal brilliance, the raw colours of childhood's spectrum
Over the yellow linoleum of the kitchen table hangs an electric bulb with a vivid green glass shade
The poker players wear coloured shirts, solid blues, a purple, a red-and-white check, a light green – they are men at the peak of their physical manhood, coarse and direct
            powerful as the primary colours
There are vivid slices of watermelon on the table, whiskey bottles and glasses

FUN AND GAMES: *Set in darkness. Crash against the front door.* MARTHA's *laughter heard.*
                Front door opens, lights are switched on.

MARTHA *enters,*   *followed by* GEORGE.

V

- A country road.
- A tree.
- Evening.

VI

Mac the Knife takes leave of his wife
and flees from his father-in-law
to the heaths of Highgate.

VII

There is a feeling of emptiness.

That night Peachum prepares his campaign. He plans to
disrupt the Coronation by a demonstration of human misery.
The beggars paint little signs with inscriptions such as
I gave my eye for my king

The view through the big windows is fading
gradually into a still-golden dusk.

Two finished kites – their artwork still unseen – lean against
the garden seat.

This poem is made up almost entirely of direct quotes from a series of canonical plays.

GLORIA HUWILER

was born and raised in Zambia to a Zambian/
British mother, and Swiss father. She pursued
acting, training at the Oxford School of Drama,
followed by achieving a BA at Brown University
and an Mst in Creative Writing from Cambridge
University. When she began writing poetry,
she found it to be cathartic in the wake of the
loss of her brother. Her poetry touches
on themes regarding identity as a
woman of colour.

NOTHING CHANGES

Trains meant pastures, manure scented,
           dawn glinting off Lake Geneva to the left,
soberly ascending mountains,
           as glacially frigid winter
released herself in rivers.
           Your laugh at the absurd detachment
of London tube announcements,
           "due to person under the train,
your carriage has been delayed."
           We couldn't sit in one afterwards.
A fever rose up my spine at the police call
           forcing me to pull over into rising red dust;
anger, at dinner plans interrupted, staring at
           the ambivalent face in the passenger seat,
dusk sucking the orange into deep indigo.
           The lights passing. What now?
We're all exhausted.
           I thought she'd collapse and wither
in a fit of hysteria, instead
           "We'll just have to get through this."
Mummy must be a phoenix.
           I'm on the rails again, eyes on the
horizon, fighting this growing nausea.
           Bra-strap constricting, a second prison grate,
as ribs cage the beasts birthed of this pounding
           bomb counting down, as we cower at
the approaching hour of freedom.
           This is just another straitjacket.
Is the call between a tranquilizer dart and the whirling
           circus roar of a wit you no longer trust a choice?
Police-men standing at the gates of mouths & hands & legs,
           at a loss, living in fear of the escape of wild things?

Would I sew treacherous lips & snaking limbs
                  to the railway lines and beg for swift obliteration?
At Christmas I bring a new baby to my
                 mouth and beg for absolution in her kiss;
hope that she swallows this hollow whole.
                We exchange gifts & glühwein.
I suppose nothing has changed.

                We've been like this for years.

NATASHA HUYNH

is a 19-year-old Vietnamese Irish-
American poet. Writing has provided her a
home in a constantly changing world, and
she hopes to give that to others too. She is an
advocate for mental health and has been featured
in Christopher Sedgwick's *Pluviophile: A Poetry
Collective*. Huynh is currently working as co-
editor of the aforementioned collective for their
2021 edition and her work has also been
featured in RDW's 'Poetry 365' for the
July, September, and October
editions.

THE DEATH OF A DREAMER

I burnt out
like a fading star in Hollywood;
my chipped and mismatched tiles
strewn together by passersby
walking on towards hopeful dreams.

The past captured
my every move
and buried my future
along with it;
what cursed bones
my casket will keep –
the life of a dreamer
too afraid
to dream.

THOMAS IRVINE

lives in Hitchin, Hertfordshire, and works at the British Library, while co-running a spoken word evening called 'Shout or Whisper'. He received his BA in English and American Literature from the University of Leicester, and graduated from the University of East Anglia with an MA in Creative Writing Poetry. Irvine has been published *in Ink, Sweat and Tears, The New Luciad, Streetcake Magazine,* and *Bridge: The Bluffton University Literary Journal.*

SOFT MACHINE (IN SUMMER SKIN)

humid saccharine on cheek; motherfuss.   a spiteful of dandelion parachutes, a
blackbird philharmonic, watertaste from   outside tap. nobody   then everybody
knows pedal without further graveling elbow scores.   your driveway an
incline   takes a little longer, everyone else leaves;   giggles distantly. instead alone,
spinning wheels upturned, prick a finger between spokes,   throb.   chalk mural
pavement washed away by a Wednesday; whole cul-de-sac cries.   only way to
wring out grass stains from forearm is via snakebite,   girl next door draws blood.

once, someone said smoke lives in between friction and twigs,   all you did was skin
away to a sage underbelly,   felt cruel. have you ever shattered a paper plate? unsure what it is
about wine   makes men cry, mantra-ing all over your shoulder *remember what young
feels*. you don't know it by anything yet, other than dockleaf soothe,   a few
summers later, wine-inspired, a whole August will be ruined by a wrong someone kissing your
eyelid closed for   first time. sports car with no middle seatbelt; lean into
corners, braced a natural state;   somehow feels right to die on a Sunday. burnt cd copy
of jumpy and scratch, red and orange songs.   a balloon escapes through sunroof as family
unisongasp. *so long, farewell, auf wiedersehen, goodbye*,   almost everybody laughing.

JOY JAMES

lives in London, England with her
family and holds a degree in Business. She
currently works at a university in London, and
has previously worked for the BBC as well as
government agencies. James recently started
writing non-fiction children's books to help
educate and inform curious young minds.
Her first book, *101 Black Inventors and their
Inventions*, will be published in 2021, and
'Melanin' is her first published poem.

MELANIN

Melanin
Is more precious than gold
Something
You've never been told

It's a secret
Not to be known
It's in tales
Not to be spoken

If you have it
You'll be hated
The jealousy
Is not overrated

Heed these words
From long and far
Read your history
And know who you are

CHRISTOPHER M. JAMES

is a dual British/French national,
retired Human Resources professional, musician
and translator. He has recently been published
in *Aesthetica*, *Ink Sweat & Tears*, *Orbis*, *London
Grip*, *DreamCatcher*, amongst others. James
was awarded first prize at the Sentinel Literary
Quarterly Poetry Competition 2020, the Maria
Edgeworth Literary Award 2019 and has won
prizes from The Stroud Book Festival, Wirral
Poetry Competition, Yeovil Literary Prize and
Poets meet Politics.

SIGUR ROS PLAY HEYSATAN ON THE WILD ICELANDIC COAST

I have to be taut, unyielding,
                                    like old rope
gnarling fingers to good account –
as lobstermen tug on credit from a lobotomy of ocean –

or be like
the pane-less windows
                        light has emptied from,
to be armed to the teeth at Selàrdalur.
Filled-in doors of earlier dreams
                                    wall me up too:
such dreams
before the ocean beat rocks
                                    into stone-deaf.

A settlement,
outlying in acres of mind,
            a far stretch
            of any imagination,
                                    watchful
of whatever sign of motion.

I was there,
smarting in the wind with wavering Arctic harebells,
                        buildings collaged
                        against colossal dusk.

They play in thick coats:
                        a bottled-up voice, six chords,
                        a harmonium,
the brass and heads

     nodding to the iron crosses —
    stories, once —
which slant to earth.

Is there anything left to life but listening?
To end up hearing yourself think.
      No edges, no off limits,
    a headland drowning
    in mist,
a body in mind.

The wind is phonemes
slurring drunk

      or dropping
      like an elapsed memory
of a thrown flask.

Don't search then
    beyond obsidian, tholeiite
    or orphan rock stacks;
all those senses compounded

      are senseless

and black Thykkvibaer beaches are but blotting paper
draining away my footprints,
      where
   the ocean places a twisted root
   one momentary day,
washes away
all seemly intent,
      the very next.

ANNA ROSE JAMES
(she/her)
is a queer, bisexual actor-writer
of mixed British and Asian heritage, based in
North Yorkshire, England. As well as poetry, she
writes short stories, fiction, memoir and scripts
for stage and screen. Her works include *Unknown*
(Stairwell Books, 2021); *Little Irritants* (Analog
Submission Press); *Love, Alberta*; *Wayside*; *100
Friggin' Poems*, *It's Ok To Fall For Camp Boys*. Her
work has been featured in *330 Words*, *Alpha Female
Society*, *Bi Women Quarterly*, *Blue Animal Literature*,
Calm Down Magazine and *Mookychick,* amongst
others.

WHEN I CALL YOUR NAME, I AM NOT ANGRY

For Beatrice Merida Kimberley Curry

Your name is a celebration

        a triumph.

It is glee it is love
        is a bird escaping a hat
it is
        a miracle.

When I call your name, I am not angry:

It is to be treasured,
        be relished,
        a blanket to wrap you in,
it is, every part of it.

Your name is not a scold,
        it is not an insult is not rage
        is not a disappointing choice made –

    a text

When I call your name,
             I see skies from mountain tops
                    I see flying I see
           wings
              I see
              Australia

I travel.

Your name,
it is source it is food,
        you are   suste-
nance.
When I call your name,

        I am fed

            and asking to feed you.

ARUN JEETOO

is an English teacher from North London.
His words appear in *The London Reader*, and in
a gallery based in Cardiff with *LUMIN Journal*.
He was a participant in Waterloo Press'
LIT UP: Poets of Colour mentoring scheme,
2019, where his debut pamphlet *I Want to Be
the One You Think About at Night* was published
(WaterlooPress, 2020). Instagram @g2poetry

THE DEATH OF PATROCLUS

On Wynne Road (SW9)
His blood slinks through
The gaps of winter pavements –
A red angel,
Euphorbos's knife
Charged
His stomach,
The liver pierces
Inhales London's befouled air.

A handful of spectators
On their balconies
Look on
From Mount Olympus estate.

The Ash tree,
By his head, a shrine for the youths
That fought with him
A shrine to lament.

Armour that could not serve or protect,
His golden ring gifted to Achilles
Weeps
An ill-fated spell.

Police scatter crowds away,
Paramedics numb to another
Fresh-limbed youth vanquished

By the concrete jungle.

His eyes cast out of light,
And the postcode war continues
Without an end in sight.

152

DONALD JENKINS

is a performance poet, writer and
spoken word promoter based in Newcastle-
upon-Tyne. He received a distinction for poetry
in his MA for Creative Writing and currently
organises and hosts Born Lippy, a live lit night
showcasing the finest national and local poets,
comedians and rappers. Jenkins won the Great
Gateshead Slam 2018 and was a semi-finalist
in the Great Northern Slam 2017. He has also
performed at Glastonbury Festival and the Royal
Albert Hall. His poems have been published in
New Word Order, The Writer's Cafe and *Riggwelter*
journal.

ODE TO MDMA (SHULGIN'S LEGACY)

You gave weekends meaning.
Kindred bore on backs
of rubs, hugs, off-lip encounters.
Palmed pleasure points discovered,
not of lovers, just every soul
inside – my mate.

You enabled faces exchanged,
painted just like mine-buckled,
chewing their merry go rounds,
gum companies kept in business
by joker packs
pulling permutations
worthy of horse collar frames.

You were my orator, joyfully
spouting cod-shit, finding out
everyone was fluent.
A tap left on, saturating
confidence, dripping empathy,
to all who paid
your membership fee.

To injections of NRG,
breaking speed limits
in shape dishing space arenas,
hearts pumping at rates of
0-300. To forever finding the
solution to the kick-drum
conundrum, only one answer –
let limbs speak loudest.

To celebrating your gender
transformation from Adam
to Mandy, Malcolm to Molly,
appearances while diverse,
have been copied such that
brands of capitalism are
forever indebted to your
torso. You provided free
product placement.

Your taste,
like fermented arsehole
never gets better with age,
dislodged in throat
like sherbet's evil twin.
I preferred you dressed
whole or halved,
digesting your aftermath
in quaking pallet.

To your Stepfather Sasha,
his vision, your primary test subject
for chemicals catalysing
mind and spirit. Re-concocting
you, a no-calorie Martini
from train-trips to Reno
to bonding broken marriages
till the comedown kicked in.

Now cultures worldwide
celebrate emotional communion
on jubilant floors
in after-hours, unadulterated,
pleasure-troves. To you,
a devotion, they're happy
to share.

BREDA JOYCE

has been shortlisted for the
Anthony Cronin, the Kinsale Festival and
Over the Edge Awards, the Fish Lockdown prize
2020 and commended in the Fool for Poetry
Chapbook competition 2019 and 2020. She won
The Judith Aronson competition UCC, 2018.
Joyce's poetry appears in *Poems for Pandemia*, *The
Honest Ulsterman*, *Kilkenny Broadsheet*, *Crannóg*,
Crossways, *Skylight 47*, *Bangor Literary Journal*, *The
Quarryman*, *The Galway Review,* and *The Waxed
Lemon*, amongst others. Her first collection
Reshaping the Light will be published in 2021
(Chaffinch Press).

NO GARDEN OF EDEN

I take my banishment willingly,
welcome all that is untamed
outside these garden walls.

I open my arms to bouquets of foxgloves
whipped by a northern wind,
gather cowslips trampled in a herded field,
unchain daisies that cower low in ditches.

I bend and hold the fractured china cup
that fell from the dresser when the dancing
thumped; I admire the stains,
the swirling cracks that remain.

I welcome the storm at sea
                              that lashes the pier,
walk closer to the edge
                         than considered wise,
unhook my anchor
                  and row furiously from the cove.

In an unsound harbour,
I set up camp not caring what's in store
and enjoy the sweetest of apples.
I am shameful no more.

TOM KELLY

lives in London, and currently works as a
laboratory technician. In 2015, he won the
Templar Portfolio Award, and his pamphlet
The Hoopoe at the execution, Villebois launched at
the Derwent Poetry Festival. In 2017, he won
The Interpreter's House open competition, and
his work has been published in several literary
magazines, including *Envoi*, *Strix* and *The
Frogmore Papers*.

THE TRANSCRIBER

I am stuck half way across the bridge in Prizren –
a town I've never visited.
The lowest layer of the cassette is always the hiss,
and radio telescopes tell us that this noise
is inescapable as it is the sound
of the heat from the birth of the universe
from which we are all refugees.

> *The smoke was like a chalk drawing at a distance,*
> *then it was like steam off a hot spring.*

I want to catch every word –
about stowing away, dehydration,
that is to say the fear to drink,
all the way back to the bridge
where I am trapped, in Prizren.
I recall how you wept, but it sounds
different now, second hand.
I listen through the noise of a café.

> *I drank from the Shadervan,*
> *and this means –*

We made each conversation into a free meal.
Cups clash, coffee grounds are tapped out,
machines captured making froth
are like accelerating steam engines.
I am still on the bridge as they pull away,
as friends laugh and call for the music
to be turned up, ask the waiter
for more house red.

> *I drank from the Shadervan,*
> *and this means I am sure to return.*

I listen for the quiet sound of a man
being dragged by a length of blue rope.
I recall the conversation, know the words
I should be hearing as I watch the road,
rewinding, reeling it back, straining again.
In your old life you were a teacher.
The hiss of the universe is inescapable.
In the restaurant nobody turns to look.

DOROTHY LAWRENSON

is a Dundee-born poet, educated in
Texas and Edinburgh, where she now resides.
Her work has been published in *South, Gutter,
Edinburgh Review, Irish Pages, Lallans* and *Painted,
spoken,* as well as in anthologies including *A Year
of Scottish Poems, Best Scottish Poetry, Be the First
to Like This, Double Bill,* and *Whaleback City.*
Lawrenson won the 2019 Wigtown
Scots Poetry Prize.

SNOW DAY

We set up the turntable and returned
to bed. Plans and warnings were judged
wanting and whited-out, like the selves
we blurred under bedclothes, insulated
four flights above the muffled streets.
Down and up were anyhow abolished
as snow swooped in arcs, or spiralled
like flakes in a shaken paperweight.
The stylus reached the centre and we let it
ride the lock-groove for an hour, laying
its crackle under peaks and troughs
of ragged breath, neither confessing
nor refuting a belief in endlessness,
just letting the noise of silence loop.

KATHERINE LOCKTON

is co-editor of *South Bank Poetry,* and
co-edited an anthology of new Scottish war
poems titled *Like Leaves in Autumn.* She has won
a number of awards including the Inaugural
International Travel Bursary by The Saltire
Society and British Council Scotland, as well
as being shortlisted for Girton College's Jane
Martin Poetry Prize; she won first place in the
Outstanding in the Field Poetry Competition.
Lockton's work has been published in *The
Glasgow Review of Books, Northwords Now,
Magma, The Spectator,* and *PN Review,*
amongst others.

DREAMS OF FALLING

My mami wraps me in an aguayo,
packs me into its colours as tightly
as minced meat tucked into an empanada.
She pulls up her pollera, then throws
me from my aunt's seventh floor window.
She does this because I'll fall anyway.

I am alone with only an open window
and seven floors to fall from for company.
I am falling towards my brother in London.
I am falling for the sweet seller's baby.
I am following her down the street as I fall.
I am as small as my mother's black doll
whose head broke off and never got fixed.

SIMON MADDRELL

was born in the Isle of Man
in 1965; after 20 years in London, he
moved to Brighton & Hove in 2020. Maddrell
writes as a queer Manx man, thriving with HIV.
His debut chapbook *Throatbone* was published
by UnCollected Press, USA in July 2020 and
Queerfella was Joint Winner in The Rialto Open
Pamphlet Competition, 2020.

WHIMBERRY PIE

Scrambling, stumbling, stooping
across remote camouflaged moor
searching with military precision for sweet dark berries.

No-one goes home until our heavy brass bucket is full
summer tasks of tiny whimberries often lasted until dusk
when soft shadows sprinkled over our pink smiling faces
cool evening air breezed across our bare bronzed arms and legs
each hair tingling with expectant thoughts of what was to come.

Golden-brown crispy pie deluged in sun-yellow custard
warm and melting like my joy-drenched heart tinged with crust.

When the summer berries were over along with apple blossoms
worlds both old and new collided like tangled brambles in my mind.
It was the autumn of our content despite those things that were not.

It was the season of pudding crumbles
fed by red-blushed Bramley's and
every ripe black-berried hedgerow we could possibly find.
Purple-stained, crimson-pricked hands eager to finish the job.

Like Grandpa
in his workshop with well-oiled, blood-stained knuckles
grasping his hammer and tongs where fountain pen once was.

Or Dad's nimble fingers tinkling his computer key board whilst
his blue eyes twinkled in the green screen light of the night.
Palms hardened by fruitful labours growing in his small field
there because now, no kids are left to go and pick them wild.

Or me, building sand dams with cracked nails so full of cement,
saving water, soil, our life-blood, otherwise lost to them.
My notebooks brim-full of verses about futures long gone,
handfuls of sweet peas, and pink roses, fuchsia, long grass.

Knowing that nothing lasts forever not even the past
the only thing I have for sure is the time I have left.
Right now, it's my whimberry pie, then I will savour the rest.

MIRVAT MANAL

is a British Somali writer and poet.
Her work has been published or is forthcoming
in *Leon Literary Review*, *Cabinet of Heed* and *101
Words*. She performs her poetry at spoken word
events, and her work is inspired by her diasporic
upbringing in the UK. Manal's work touches
on topics that include race relations, female
empowerment, self-acceptance, as well as other
topics that revolve around identity. Twitter
@MirvatManal Instagram @mirvatmanal

AFRICAN BURN

Sore from the clutches of an African burn,
The firm twist of expectance,
The rough hands of the bread winner sinking in.
Palms battered in white and sweat,
His father made mud cakes,
He made bread,
Now it's time I made pastries.

Elbows scratched,
Dragged towards a subservient existence,
Down a narrow, culturally embellished corridor with no end,
Pass the hanging dambiil basket,
Kicking over the camel-skin, gumbar stool.

I have to make them proud at an invisible cost,
Plunging down on a sharpened sword,
Still stained with my predecessor's blood.
But this has kept many before me alive and full.
Head tilting, the response is in limbo,
So the submission begins,
Lies that even the spinner believes.

RAIF MANSELL

is a poet from Liverpool, and is
currently working on a collection called *Poems
for Tyrants*. He has been published in *3:am*, and
has collaborated in numerous Enemies readings
in addition to presenting work in the Museum
of Futures: Visual Poetry exhibition.

A POEM FOR TYRANTS

Sculpture isn't for young men, they are themselves
Everything, wearing white vests in the blueprints of buildings.
Scores, angles, create a body's climate, not the eyes as a megamerger
To total them. Tyrants make love to men by using their tips
To mold the image they're caressing; a cheekbone disposing of sorrow
Depends on even the smallest of matter
Keeping pace. What is unexplainable statistically, is style.
One exact universe dilating is style, the past draining the present
Is style. Dylan Rieder has its mouth, asking you where you are,
Against your ear and you're replying *gone, gone*. And style
Is feeling that you are gone, not him, and style has you taking his steps
Across the mirrors of your forehead, and if a soul dares to utter
Please, he is its answer, and style is the sheer lostness when he is not you,
Nor her. Tyrants miss only what they know they will never fuck,
        conquer, become.

MARIE MAYINGI

is 20-years-old, and was born in Paris,
France before moving to England. She is
currently reading English Law and French Law
at the University of Exeter. She has previously
published two poetry chapbooks, *Ravings,* 2018,
and *Happier,* 2019, and her first play, *Antigone*
has been or is forthcoming to be performed as
part of the Philadelphia Artists' Collective's
New Venture Festival in February 2021 and B3's
Theater's Annual Festival of Shorts throughout
Summer 2021.

SENSE

i tried to play sense into you
but i'm not familiar with that sound

as i felt my way in your bosom
i plucked your ribs,
and beat your heart like a drum.

your lungs would shrink and violently burgeon
                             under my touch.
the strident cry of devotion,
a deadly rush

i tried to play sense into you,
i let it echo all around

and when i was content with the sound,
still you were mute, and i was blind

NICHOLAS McGAUGHEY

is a Literature Wales mentee.
His work appears in *Poetry Wales, The Ogham Stone, Ink Sweat and Tears, Prole* and *The Poetry Archive,* amongst others. 'Buying A Camper' was first published in the *Beyond The Storm* anthology (Write Out Loud, 2020).

BUYING A CAMPER

Craned under the cranked up chassis,
we pored over mud-salt,
struts and welds,
the iron bowel of the beast
tanked and riveted,
rust-pocked-chrome-plated
sumped and treacly:
the sum of a million revolutions
and the brunt of twenty sandy seasons
bounced on the axle of its dinted shell;
its grille and headlights smiling still.

And this old van came rolling home
on a cold January day
to take us to our summers.

It sits where I parked it in the frost,
furloughed in a street of starers,
gathering moss and the quiet bunting of spiders,
blinded by pollen and petal
with wheels turned out towards the sea.

JAMES McGOVERN

received a BA in English and a
Master's in Creative Writing from Oxford
University. He is currently Senior Editor at
the *Oxonian Review* and Advisory Editor for
Creative Writing Studies at Vernon Press.
His poetry and prose have appeared in several
venues, including *Prospect* magazine and *The
Oxford Review of Books*. In 2019, his narrative
nonfiction piece 'The Truth' was longlisted
for the *Australian Book Review's*
Calibre Essay Prize.

THE CHIAROSCURIST

Ah the skill of that Florentine   with dampened paper, sheets of copper or zinc

sulphur, clay or lampblack   the etcher's trusty staples, who with her needle

figures illusion's depths   with something like the magic of the forger

the hollows filling with enamel   summoning shifty Merlin, sweet Nimue

the shady parts crosshatching   beneath the misty Eastern heavens

or a girl's slender shadow on a stair   plea of beauty in a darkened doorway

pearls upon the shore   orblights swirling in the opiate boughs

or twisted briars and brambles   the queen and her rose soft menacing

to draw a rainawakened daisy   nudged into being by a blade of grass

pouring such ink over the jewels of time   to preserve them in night's dreamless keep

SIGHLE MEEHAN

is a winner of the 2018 iYeats International
Poetry Competition. She has been widely
published by *Poetry Ireland Review, The Stinging
Fly, Crannóg, Skylight 47, Fish Anthology, Magnum
Opus* (New Delhi), and elsewhere. Meehan was a
runner-up for Over The Edge New Writer 2018,
came third for The McLellan Poetry Prize 2018
and was a finalist for the Shirley McClure Poetry
Prize 2018.

ICARUS IN DONEGAL

Wings made by his father
left him free to fly,
he imagined marble towers, spires
that touched the sun,
he imagined skies so wide
they clothed the world
in blue, he imagined beaches
where the sand was warm, the water
tinged with sapphire.

His father welded
the wingspan of his dreams,
he saw himself a merchant, new-age
on the silk routes, snuffling spices,
perfumes, pearls,
he saw himself on telly
interviewing sports stars,
he saw himself in Brussels
Commissioner for Hand-Outs.

His father urged him spread his wings,
travel, university,
winter sun glanced shadows
on the Swilly, scorched
the vastness as daylight peeled,
traced his name in Ogham
on an ice-age sea,
midnight settled on a purple pier.

He heard the honk of whooper swans,
heard music down in Deeney's pub
songs he could not bundle

179

in a back-pack
thought
he'd go before the Lent
maybe after Paddy's Day
he'd go in early summer

he'd go next year.

FRED MELNYCZUK

is a writer based between Scotland and London, and he is currently studying for an MLitt Creative Writing at the University of Glasgow. He has had book reviews, articles, poems and stories appear in several publications internationally; the UK, Holland, and the US, including *The Poetry Review, the FT, The Telegraph,* and *The London Magazine.* In 2018, he was shortlisted for the Alpine Fellowship Writing Prize.

UN SUEÑO

It's the quiet hush of midnight... no ripple, or murmur to it.

We have enveloped the other; and with the wonder
of a baby's hand, I touch her lips, and watch, her tender pulse.

'Listen', she whispers, 'yours beats like a drum
and mine a whisper; am I really living?'
But I have never
seen such a living thing;
she who wears perfection like a perfume.

I've never
seen such a place as this: the deserts of the south,
the mountains of the north; these days of frenzied music
and sun-bleached stone; these hot nights,
wedged between the alleys that burrow into the darkness.

★ ★ ★

In this dream I speak softly, the fine balance of her name,
and I love in wonder, the gaze of her eyes,
on such holy nights when I would rest on her, and her on me...

AUDREY MOLLOY

is an Irish poet based in Sydney, Australia.
Her work has appeared in *The North, Mslexia,
Magma, Poetry Ireland Review, The Moth, The Irish
Times* and *Southword*. In 2019 she received the
Hennessy Award for Emerging Poetry as well
as the Aesthetica Creative Writing Award and
the An Post Irish Book Award (APIBA) for Irish
Poem of the Year. www.audreymolloy.com

ON REACHING 45 THE POET REALISES SHE IS ONLY 23

It happened quite by accident, snipping a loose thread from the hem of my corset, the blade nicked my thigh and the tiny wound ran round my leg tin-opener fashion. Not a drop of blood spilt, but my flesh rippled to the ground like a silk stocking freed from its garter on a close afternoon. Beneath, a taut and muscular thigh, covered in a gleaming coat of black hair. I was less shocked than you might imagine, thrilled, in fact, to make this discovery, so I set about freeing the rest of the leg. The ankle was a real sticking point and I had to sit on the floor, prising away flesh with a cheese knife, a box cutter for the tendons, tougher than steel, until there, on the parquetry, lay a coal-black neat and polished hoof. I was quicker with the second leg, applying lessons from the first. Already I could feel a surge of life through my veins, a snort in my nostrils. The gloves of my tired arms peeled away to new limbs of chestnut brown with willowy hands and fingernails like dogwood petals. Flaying the torso was painful, but how proud I was of my high round breasts, my belly rippling where it met the pelt reaching up to my waist. *You sexy fuck*, I whispered to the creature in my bathroom mirror, then grabbed each ear and pulled upwards. A lake of hair fell over my shoulder and down to my navel. My eyes were ringed with black paint, my mouth, cleft as a hare. This was no dream, I tell you; this was just the beginning. In my zeal I trod on my tail three times before draping it over my arm and, grabbing my best bag and throwing in the knives, I was off to where the wild ones go to dance among the boabs.

STEPHEN JAMES MOORE

was born in Hertfordshire, England,
and currently resides in Bristol. He has
previously studied in Newcastle-upon-Tyne
and Brighton, and currently works in a cardiac
catheterisation suite. His instagram handle is
@stephen_james_moore

DIAGNOSTIC ANGIOGRAM

We shave you
just a corner we say
then we check for
allergies on your wrist
stained like fake tan, orange
make an insertion
for the tube, six French
a push, a twist, penetrated
dark red flash back, then
a burn, our own special cocktail
the wire will creep up you
into your very soul
your aortic arch curls over
obscene like canine lipstick
then, all your heart is exposed
for all to see and know.

BETH MORRISON

currently resides in East London. She has a BA in Creative Writing and has previously studied screenwriting, art and drama.

THE NORTH IN WINTER

The gull's cawing calls slice up the sky,
sharp as the iron land they inhabit.
There is no dusk apparent,
in the afternoon, the moon.
Then darkness.

Only the sea birds on the cliff face
can make it their home.
And the owls with their flutey calls
that perch on the rooftops.
And there's always roadkill,
hares dash rashly for cover.

Rain blows in from the North,
it hammers at the windows
 in diagonals tipped with ice.
There is a low accompaniment
in the distance like a breath;
a steady exhalation, of the sea.

It crashes its foamy whites upon the shore
with such beguiling constancy,
dissembling its depths.

OLIVER MORT

is from Belfast, and has been published in *Envoi, Poetry Ireland Review, Poetry Salzburg Review, The Rialto, Scintilla, Wasafiri*, and elsewhere. Mort has previously been longlisted for the Alpine Fellowship, 2019 Writing Prize and his work has been included in the Seamus Heaney Award for *New Writing Anthology, 2019*, and more recently *Places of Poetry: Mapping the Nation in Verse*, (Oneworld Publications, 2020).

IN 1987

we unplugged from Belfast's mad game
of *Tetris*, stuck a Nintendo into the electric for fun
and played *Super Mario Brothers*
until our hands felt completely numb.

Mario and Luigi raced from left
to right across the old Panasonic TV screen
smashing the brick blocks
where question marks had been

and all the Koopa Troopas or Paratroopas
in the world couldn't inhibit
our progress. Except for all the checkpoints
and pitfalls and the stupid time limit.

ANDREW GEOFFREY KWABENA MOSS

is a writer and teacher who has lived in
the UK, Japan and currently, in Australia.
Of Anglo-Ghanaian heritage, his work seeks
to explore and challenge liminal landscapes,
complex identities and the social constructs of
race. He has previously had work published by
*Afropean, People in Harmony, Fly on the Wall Press,
Fair Acre Press, Red Penguin Books, Scissortail Press,*
and *dyst Literary Journal,* amongst others.

MY GOLDEN COAST

Part One
As a child I flexed my mother's tongue
Asante Twi,
On dusty laterite compound steps
Fading Portuguese façades and colonial schemes
An Empire of broken dreams

Ghana,
What do you mean to me?
What do you owe to me?

A romanticised vision convinced me
Of a royal return *Roots* and all
An answer to Haley's clarion call

Fufu pounds,
Plantain fries
Bringing contented sighs as family abounds

In '77 cold English skies
Froze hitherto our sun-drenched African lives
Sounds and memories slowly evaded

Sanguine hopes of another me shaded
'What is Ghana like?' I quizzed my mother
In a Bedfordshire tongue
In a market town garden was I led up the path
Kept in the dark?

Part Two
I cried tears for this faraway treasured land
My Gethsemane awaited
The dreams would not subside

I pictured a warm embrace and *Akwaaba*
Or was this an ill-fitting fiction?
Set up against the backdrop of Thatcher's theatrical Britain
Riots and miners' strikes
What is your fate when two cultures collide?
Was I to become a vultured victim?

Touch-down to reality in the 1990's,
Surprise
Landing upon Ghanaian soil
A blanket of warmth embroils
That first African night the talking drumbeats pound
Undulating tribal voices reverberate, confound
New sounds envelop
So many blacks:
Red black, blackcurrant black, plum black, blueberry black
Greet the whites of my eyes.

On a new continuum of colour I am seen as *Obroni*
A white in their lives

Disoriented in a dark room of negative perception

In Britain I am black
In Ghana I am white
The realisation of the Middle way is born,
Shades of grey unhinge my door.

193

D.M. O'CONNOR

has an MFA from University College
Dublin as well as from the University of New
Mexico. He is a contributing reviewer for *Rhino
Poetry* and fiction editor at *Bending Genres* and
his work has appeared in *Splonk, A New Ulster,
Cormorant, Crannog, Opossum, The New Quarterly,*
and *The Guardian,* amongst others. He is the
recipient of the 2021 Cúirt International
Award for Fiction.

A STUDY OF LAW & ORDER

The boys dragged him from the footpath by the hair.

They didn't like his sound.

Used bike-chains as knuckle dusters,

liver punched to mask bruise history.

Burning pallets sparkle under cloud siege

hide any illusion to any North Star.

Costumed as cop, a cameo, a career, Babyface says,

Things get rough snowflake, move it along.

Skin burst, smell kindles truncheon imaginings.

195

Three million doorlocks latch simultaneously.
Not a call placed. No memory to witness.
This horror is nothing   new.

What do we have here?
Call the blood guy.
Cordon it off.
Keep the cameras away.

At this point the judge turned to the child psychologist and
asked for a personal opinion. The nuns had testified. A native
Huron smoked signals. Dictionary extinct. All deer wept as the
gavel paused in mid-air.

Hesitation is often about money.
          Later, rapture approaching,
                    grandmothers hum,
                              rake all the ash into the lake.

KEVIN O'KEEFFE

was born in Ireland, and currently lives in
America. He is a mathematician as well as a poet
and his work has been featured in *Page & Spine*.

EXPATRIATE

Oh quiet little Irish boy
for all your tasseled talents
you know not what you do.

It took the mis-
givings of a foreign public
to get you to think

and now with limber
tinder-thumbs
you're off

to another land of anonymity
gold with hope.
But roots won't fix

in moving soil.
The spice of the new
won't keep a season

and you know too well
the empty aftershock of novelty,
those long and

maudlin months of nothinghood,
the gloom of isolation,
the char of wrong.

Are you more sturdy
this time round?
Have you the skin for the black-

blank expanse
of life gone wrong?
The tasing certainty of error?

Have you forgotten the
cracked chin? The low
rumble of dysfunction

as you, troubled and joy-sore,
kissed the cusp of ruin?
You've learned by book

and by blister
that it takes a village to
think – who will let you in?

Unskinny and thirty –
odd and alone? The shallow
charlantry of

boy-charm, once,
the very pulse of merriment,
reeks like fish.

The date is out of such be-foolery
and you're stocked with little else.
Think an adult minute:

does sun
and a jump in class
measure more than country and clan?

Than a crop of true friends
won over by
time – and by time alone?

I see those riddling
sleights of mind as you
run,

cap and cowlick,
from the hurt in your skull.
Sticky verities.

Ridless grins.
O feeble Irishman,
this awesome

privilege of liberty
was meant for backs
far broader than yours.

You'll crack by forty.
They'll come with a box
and shove in your invalid

muscles, rot-rank,
and ship you right back to the
start! —

tangled patriot,
guilty traveler,
thick hick.

ROUA OUBIRA

currently resides in London, where she studies Creative Writing at Brunel University. Her work has been published in *Robots, Rogues and Revenants* anthology and she won first place in Brunel University's Winter Poetry contest, 2020.

*خولة بنت الأزور

She brought the tent down on its knees
Took its skinny pegs between her palms
Her coarse fingers commanded that they spun liberty. And they did.
Ground their haystack of pride, weaved it into gilded skin. So that it
flaked
And flames
Of confetti flew around in   the rakish air.
like
petals
of
a
thorny,
weary rose. She brought the girls up from their knees
Took their skinny arms and commanded that
they too should spin.

* **Khawlah bint al-Azwar:** a Muslim warrior during the life of the Islamic Prophet Muhammed (PBUH) and later a military leader. She once was imprisoned by Byzantine soldiers amongst other women and fought her way to freedom with only tent poles.

MHAIRI OWENS

lives in Fife, Scotland, and is a
community worker in addition to tutoring
poetry for the University of St Andrews
International Summer School. Her poems have
appeared in various anthologies and journals
including *Cyphers, Glasgow Review of Books,
Ink, Sweat and Tears, Poetry Salzburg Review,
Southlight, Strix, The Moth, The North* and
The Rialto. 'When Darwin Didn't Discover
Morrough' was originally published by
ProleBooks. Owen's poem 'Shiftin' won
the 2019 Wigtown Prize, the first
ever Scots entry to do so.

WHEN DARWIN DIDN'T DISCOVER MORROUGH

None of this is new. I was a specimen way back
when *The Beagle* berthed at *Eilean nam Ban Mora.*

It took him a full day to haul the length of me from *The Well*
as you'd expect, extended metaphor that I'd become.

Barren he heard, and *One-trick* – tinkling against the deck
from my pelvis down. *Hmm*, he brain-stormed.

Naturally, select words have acted as an enzyme
to conjoin the legs and have here overlapped,
over time, into this scaly armour. Seemingly,
supremely adapted to its circumstances, this is…

Anathema to his theory then. *Fucking mermaids*
he concluded, chucking me overboard and sailing on.

Morrough | morrow/mermaid; Eilean nam Ban Mora | Island of the Big Women/
Eigg; The Well | The Green Well/the edge of the world in Gaelic mythology.

JANET PHILO

retired from an education career and
is now a writer. Based in Derbyshire, much
of her work was created in the North East,
including titles *Under-hedge Dapple* and *Cheap
Fish for Kings*, as well as work in anthologies,
including *I Bet I Can Make You Laugh* and
Midnight Feasts.

GHAZAL FOR THE CAMPERS

After Richard Mosse – photographer

It stinks – that dark and putrid pool of shitful mire. She's longing
for clear water, diamond-bright and cleaned with fire. She's longing

for the quiet sleep brings, but not the quiet of death. Despite the pain,
the sickness and an empty belly, he's still a crier – but her, she's longing

for a time she doesn't need the sound of wailing as evidence of life.
Quiet babies don't light darkness, don't desire, don't feel the longing

for the warmth of breath or breast or soft toys long forgotten.
Her baby quietens, does not cry, his eyes are drier now, too dry for longing.

Her tears, clear rivers on a dusty cheek, give thanks for one more breath,
as fingers curl round hers. Woman – God loves a trier! Keep on longing.

LAURA POTTS

is a writer from West Yorkshire,
England. She is a recipient of the Foyle Young
Poets Award, and her work has been published
by *Aesthetica, The Moth* and *The Poetry Business*.
Potts became one of the BBC's New Voices in
2017, and she received a commendation from
The Poetry Society in 2018. She was
also shortlisted for The Edward Thomas
Fellowship, The Manchester Poetry Prize
and The Bridport Prize in 2020.

THE NEVER-MOTHER

Outside my skin: cold, and stone skies. I weep
and think of hands – stressed, clenched – his skull
moulded in the crack of my elbow, and rock him,

crying, caressing the soft pearls of his eyelids.
Thunder snarls in the dead of night.
Say *light* and I swallow my stomach.

He sleeps in some other arms now, my son,
wakes to the halls of dawn in another land
far from here, where a woman will not hold him

quite like I did. The moon will be old and
the stars wheeled away before I see him, my boy,
striding with limbs long to his mother's open arms;

when the skies will flame with copper, copper, crimson
and tan. When he will stop, cold, and ask me who I am.

CIAN QUINN

is a 27-year-old native of Tipperary, Ireland, currently residing and working in Andalucia, Spain. Quinn's work has appeared in *The Ofi Press*, *The Glad Rag* and *The Dillydoun Review*.

IRELAND

After Dave's *Black*

Ireland is Ra tunes and fancy coffee
Ireland is freckles and intelligence
Ireland is disgust at the weather, yet not taking an umbrella
saying sorry for shouldering strangers in the streets
but family-feuding over that carry-on at Aisling's wedding for years after

It's racist to say Ireland is potatoes, though we do love mash and chips
and wedges and Taytos and potato gratin and roast spuds
and potato bread, of all things

Ireland is supporting sporting underdogs
heading over to The States, or Down Under to get sunburn,
singing 'The Fields of Athenry' and passing out on streets
your grand-uncle laid the concrete for

Ireland is good butter and milk
Ireland is The Great Irish Water Rebellion
Ireland is never accepting compliments without first clarifying
you got your jacket in Penney's
and saying nothing to no one about your anxiety,
or the lump in your chest that keeps you from sleeping

Ireland is speaking English, or Hiberno-English
Ireland is 20 euro for a main, but with sound service
Ireland is Bobby Sands and Bono
Ireland is the Cliffs of Moher and that Guinness ad (that was
        Michael Fassbender
who swam to America to apologise to yer man)
Ireland is a permanent 30% chance of rain
Ireland is class elitism, TDs hiking rent prices, and the equation:
        People=Scum

And hard-drinking, and craic-atoning, and póg-mo-thóining
And Christy Moore and Aisling Bea and Seamus Heaney

You know yourself what Ireland is
Ireland is
Sure look

YVONNE REDDICK

is an associate editor at *Magma* magazine, as well
as the author of *Translating Mountains, Spikenard*
and *Ted Hughes: Environmentalist and Ecopoet*. Her
poetry has appeared in *The Guardian, PN Review*
and *Poetry Ireland Review,* and she has received
a Northern Writer's Award, a Hawthornden
Fellowship, the Poetry Society's Peggy Poole
Award, a commendation in the 2018 National
Poetry Competition and a first place prize in
The Ambit Poetry Competition.

STORM PETREL

I

My father departed to raise the Jurassic.
The hill-wind on his face, before weeks
aboard the rig. North of the peak
where his path would end, he'd spent Sunday
trudging to the Nevis cairn.

The pilot made him walk a line.
"Drysuit? Lifejacket?"
– "Check."
"Reddick?"
– "Ready!"
The rotor-blades split air.
He watched cities shrinking:
Stonehaven, Peterhead,
Aberdeenshire's rain-grey granites.

Over the waves, the blade of Shetland.
They named the metal sea-lands
for birds: Merlin, Osprey, Brent.
He stepped onto the platform, for
the two-week static voyage.

2

So seabound, she stumbled on land –
tough light approaching, though
days were no longer.
Dust hazing the air, dust
in the petrel's throat and feathers;
sand clouding the sea where she dived.

213

By the rock-caves, fishermen with their catch
of conches sat on hot stones,
cracking the chambers of shells.
The Sahara had flown to
sea on the Harmattan –
the conch-fishers scarved
their eyes to watch the petrels
patter wings and feet on waves,
stepping north on water.

3

The rig-lights fiery on choppy breakers.
In his bunk, sardine-canned
with four snoring dorm-mates,
my father restive under a thin blanket.

Noise jackhammered everyone's eardrums –
drilled through cabins,
girders. Dad felt the weather turn.
The men perched

over an ocean above
a deeper ocean of sweet, black oil.
The rig boomed like a petrol tanker,
its hull pitching over the North Atlantic.

Dinner was mock chop, double chips and peas,
then double chips and peas with mock chop again.
Failure to hold the handrail
was a sackable offence.
My father learnt how
to say *No sé hablar Español*
at night classes. Workers on
an iron-and-concrete outcrop

need instructive hobbies. They miss
their women, their families, grow fractious –

4

Scavenging flotsam:
shrimps, krill, moon jellyfish,
those translucent creatures
called by-the-wind sailors.

Petrels can smell oil a mile off,
will scrounge whale blubber
or scraps from a salmon farm.

They follow in the wake of trawlers.

5

A favourite pastime is birding. Blown off course,
birds are enticed by rig-lights. They know
these angular sea-rocks
gather rainwater. One morning, the men
woke to find an osprey staring
them down from the crown block.

Other émigrés: fieldfares, bramblings,
the injured short-eared owl that flew
landward in the helicopter with the drilling crew.

A seal that surfaced and offered a sardine
to the scaffolder on the abseil line –
they locked gazes, eyes round as portholes.

The best was the corncrake,
rasping by the draw-works –

all hundred and two men
raised their glasses of Kaliber.

6

The petrel was heading for Mousa,
the crumb of rock holding
her nest in the prehistoric cairn.
She and her mate would tend
a quartz-white egg,
each parent brooding the warm, live pebble,
before the weather turned and they
returned to the Cape Verde winter.

7

Wind woke and filled its lungs.
Three-metre waves slammed the legs
of Dunlin A. The flame blown backwards
down the steel throat of the flarestack dragon.
Whiplash rain, near-horizontal.
A crackle on the intercom:
Deck's slippery, boys!

No-one slept that night: the storm bawled
through chinks in cabins, and rain
battered its fists on the roof. The rig
an ocean liner, tethered but foundering.

Bloodshot sky that morning; the blown gale sullen.
The men went on deck to hand-line for mackerel.
My father told me, with a catch
in his throat, of the disgorger,
the gaff, their dulling eyes.
A gift of slick-blue bodies for my mother

when he returned, the red
wound in each hulled belly.

8

At the first whiff of fish-guts
they arrived like a squall:
the flock treading water
to the rig with its sea-legs.

One of them crash-landed by the galley.
Draggled feathers; only her head moved,
flicking right and left in panic.
The rig cook, once a ship's chef,
offered leftover cod.
"It's a petrel. Never seen them so early.
Sailors say they bring heavy weather."

9

My father cradled the exhausted traveller,
lighter than the balsa glider he assembled
as a boy. He ran his fingers along the wiry
struts of wing-bones, checked
the ruddering tail, the submarine keel-bone
and relaunched the storm petrel
into an unsettled sky.

GUY RUSSELL

was born in Chatham, and has since
worked as a holiday courier, purchasing clerk,
media analyst and fan-heater production
operative. His writing has appeared in *The
Rialto, The Yellow Crane, The Iron Book of New
Humorous Verse* (Iron Press), *Troubles Swapped
For Something Fresh* (Salt Publishing), amongst
others. Russell has received first prize in the
Leicester Poetry competition, Flash500, Cannon
Sonnet or Not and he has also been the recipient
of the HE Bates Award. He reviews at https://
tearsinthefence.com/blog

MA IN POETRY WRITING

GENERAL PAPER 11 June 2019. THREE HOURS.
Answer FOUR questions ONLY.

1. 'Every age gets the literature it deserves.' OR 'Poetry makes nothing happen.' Discuss with reference to the work of several famous poets, and then to your own.

2. Describe at length the way in which certain key experiences in your childhood led to your decision to become a serious writer.

3. Write a *profound* 14-line poem with the line-endings: *choose, beat, eat, shoes, know, concern, learn, go, reduction, mean, obscene, seduction, breeze, trees.*

4. Remark in detail on the principal faults in the poetry of another member of the course OR Assess the benefits and disadvantages of the workshop system OR Do you think your tutor is really worth that salary? Why (not)?

5. Write an essay on any subject, naming and quoting as many French post-structuralist intellectuals as you can.

6. Explain why you should receive an Arts Council grant, and the purpose to which you would put it OR Describe why you would like to be a writer-in-residence.

7. 'Readers are the kind of people... you can sleep with' (Paterson). Discuss with reference to any ONE poet you have met OR Does heavy drinking help or hinder the aspiring writer? Illustrate your answer with anecdotes.

8. Write the blurb for your future collection.
OR
Name your Desert Island Discs. Why have you chosen them?

9. Briefly assess the potential advantages/disadvantages in your becoming: (i) a WEA creative-writing tutor (ii) a small-press magazine editor (iii) a part-time Literature Development Officer (iv) a poetry competition judge.

10. Write a (i) letter to an editor or publisher to accompany a submission (ii) letter to a well-known poet who could help your career (iii) short biog which makes you sound interesting, modest and publishable.

11. Parody ANY poem by John Ashbery as if by Paul Muldoon
OR Parody ANY poem by John Ashbery as if by John Ashbery
OR Parody ANY parody by Peter Reading by Peter Reading by Peter Reading by
OR
What *is* Postmodernism?

12. 'All poems are about poetry." OR 'Anything can be a poem.' Discuss.

KHANUM SHAAN

is a 20-year-old, British Pakistani living in the
UK. She is inspired by Faiz Ahmed Faiz, and
listens to ghazal poetry as a way of connecting
to her roots.

PALESTINE

The waves violent and raw
Forcefully ripping through all walls
The bleak sound of war

The rustle of clouds
An ear-splitting sound, bleeding her orbs
Enslaved in a place called the cage

Staring at the sky
She prays with her palms
Blocking bombs away from her face

NEELAM SHAH

achieved her Masters in Psychoanalysis
from Kingston University. She is currently
a freelance Researcher/Analyst for Fintech
Pharmaceuticals, a freelance academic health
researcher for Knowledge Links, proofreader
for London Skills Network and Adhoc Ranstad
Disability Support Worker. Shah is an e-activist,
Global Citizen Leader, and political lobbyist for
PETA, Walk for Freedom Slavery Activist, End
Global Poverty, Unicef Children's Champion,
Greenpeace, Climate Reality as well as a GQ
Transforming Mental Health Supporter.

FIRE AS WE KNOW HIM

I have heard of fire being hazardous to human,
horse, house and forest, bringing destruction
to anything that comes its way, spitting without remorse.
He is seen as a common blazing enemy,
but is that entirely his fault or are there accomplices
involved in awakening him to act this way?
I have also heard of the fire's enemies –
courageous fighters who rescue victims of his wrath,
smiting the burning lord with his two weaknesses.

I have heard of fire being talked about as
passion, desire and anger in a romance, or
being an exasperation for the poor mind.
There are also good stories of the Conflagration King.
Being a warm refuge for people who want to escape from bitter ice
inviting everyone to his heated territory, a natural furnace.
I have heard him being celebrated by the legendary magnificent
Chinese dragons who breath red, orange and yellow
as a weapon of power – for strength, might and courage.

I have seen him as symbols for prosperity, unity
and happiness at weddings, where the bride and groom
walk around him three times in a circle to keep an everlasting marriage.
He is also used in funerals, although then he takes a different name –
for this time is cremation, scorching flame, engulfing whole bodies.
He is spoken of in science lessons; he is demonstrated in a three-sided diagram
a triangle cycle, combustion, convection, insulation, which make up his body.
He helps bring two people together in the night.
I have heard of fire in a good light and a bad light.

SALLY SPEDDING

is from Porthcawl, Wales, a country where she
currently resides. She studied sculpture and
has written fifteen crime thrillers, such as
Wringland and *The Devil's Garden*. She has
twice won the International Welsh Poetry
Competition, and her first published poem,
'Cowhand', won the Forward Press £3,000
Poetry Award. www.sallyspedding.com

SEIZURE

In the derelict Oradour-sur-Glane, March 20th, 2016

A shining lake, a winding road of generous curves through Nieul,
Saint-Gence, past new-builds and a school buzzing with its carefree
young. Blowsy blossom moves on the breeze as a herd of
Limousins laze along Le Glane trickling by, and two lithe
Germans laugh in the sun, check the skis on their car roof.
A good trip done.

And then comes the village; stage of ghosts. So easy to enter. Too
easy to enter... *Bienvenue*, with nothing now to lose. Yet this could
happen all over again.
A crow pecks between tramlines and beyond an apple tree's
black-fisted branches, a neat house peeks where childhood ended
with the half-dressed doll. A top still spinning…

A tribe of teens swarms by and some happy lad mimes a scattergun
spree while a giggling girl primps her braids, singing Cher's 'I believe.'
Yet above this clamour, come the dead; their heavy breaths, their begging
prayers. For where was the priest that hot afternoon when his locked church
heaved as flares were lit?

This gilded day – the vernal equinox – with those grassy plots, the pastoral
bliss of copse and field. An affront to charred cornerstones and
doors that couldn't save a soul, nor the Café's wreck of chairs
nor the doctor's rusted car sunk on its haunches with no more
missions of mercy in the awkward hours. The silent nights…

226

My pulse has paused. I'm cold as they in the graveyard. Cold and afraid in
the shadow of a broken wall, as I wait for that same busy crow to rise.
Fly free.

The villagers of Oradour-sur-Glane were massacred by the Nazis on June 10th 1944.

LOLA STANSBURY-JONES

is a young, working-class poet from North Wales. She is currently a full-time undergraduate student, at the Open University, where she studies history, and her work has been published in print and online, in publications such as the *Atlanta Review, Down in the Dirt Magazine*, and *Friday Flash Fiction*.

THE ROLLING, DRIFTLESS NORTH

Steel mills speak to me
with messages disguised in smoke.
They bleed and wheeze before they retreat
and surrender to a blanket of snow.

They send men with tired eyes
out to place bets on feral dogs.
We begin and end in graveyards,
and sink deeper into the beyond.

Out here, on these great northern plains
where the sky will always flee from the sun
everything is beautiful
and terrible all at once.

ALEXANDRA STRNAD

read English at the University of Cambridge, and graduated with Distinction from the M.St. in Creative Writing at the University of Oxford. She is a dual Czech-British national and has previously lived in Prague. She was the 2014 Winner of the Jane Martin Poetry Prize, and a 2016 Winner of the Oxford University Parallel Universe Poetry Competition. Strnad's first poetry pamphlet, *H is for Hadeda,* was published by Poetry Salzburg, University of Salzburg, in 2017, and 'Thirsting' was originally published in *Oxford Poetry*, XVIII.I / WINTER 2018-2019.

THIRSTING

It is blond lager paired with cheap cigarettes,
noble hops aromatic beneath the smoke;

the patter of a Bichon Frise – short tongue, pink
as a rasher of bacon, pulling his lady by the lead;

the odour of dumplings in sweet, heavy sauces;
the curse of the patron as he steers his utopenec★

mouth-wards, chews down hard on mercury
capped molars; the terpene of grapes

in the vineyard at Villa Gröbe, which grows
more sulphurous at early evening, commingling

with untended honeysuckle, sweating
after the noonday glare, behind the tenement,

where lovers picnic like glasses of young wine,
purrs of laughter twinned with the racket

of bicycles on cobbles set neat as pangolin scales;
the man who leans from his window, his awkward

flirtations with any girl that passes; the sigh
of the labourer after the first sip, froth wiped

from moustache to sleeve – the day's first draught
a consolation, quenching the panic of the age.

★Czech, literal translation: 'drowned man' – a pork sausage pickled in vinegar and
typically eaten with rye bread.

WILLIAM THOMPSON

is a PhD candidate in Creative Writing
at the University of Bristol. Born in
Cambridgeshire in 1991, his work has appeared
or is forthcoming in *Wild Court, Raceme, The
Honest Ulsterman, Lighthouse, Ink Sweat & Tears,
The Cannon's Mouth* and *Atrium*.

VAULTING

The engine tapering across the sky,
at this precise instant, transforms,
becomes an emblem patterning its way
towards sheer absence. Below, its noise
is sharpened by the garden sound of birds;
the silence of my father as he sleeps
his face half in shade, his shirt unbuttoned,
his trousers rolled to just below the knee.
And for a second I could swear I feel
the dizzy glide, the paralysing swoop,
of our velocity through empty space.
And then I have the urge to wake him up,
the sudden overwhelming feeling that
I mustn't miss one second more of him.

PETER VIGGERS

gained an MA in Poetry from the
Centre for New Writing at the University
of Manchester in 2016. He is treasurer of the
Manchester based organisation Poets and
Players, who organise poetry and music events.
His poem 'Wolf Clearance' was shortlisted for
The Bridport International Poetry Prize in 2018.
Other poems have been shortlisted for The
Anthony Cronin International Poetry Award
and, highly commended in The Brian Dempsey
Memorial Prize. His poems have appeared in
Orbis International Literary Journal, *The Best of
Manchester Poets Volumes 2 & 3*, *SMOKE* and
Mancunian Ways, amongst others.

WOLF CLEARANCE

Checking out the content of his shed,
I howl and cover myself with hair
licking my father's rusty saw,
his father's fireman's axe,
paw the metal headed mallet, sniff
the claw headed hammer, crawl around
scattered tacks and boxes of screws.
Steel wool scrapes my pelt,
slink back to where I was first born,
clubbed with other cubs, avoid
the vice with its hard command.
Fearing I might be left alone
to howl without the moon
among scraps of iron, a grey chain
hanging over my head, nails stab
feet, driven from my chosen field.
I had no wish for kennels, crazed
without my pack, breath rank,
dreaming of flesh; free outside,
I lick my teeth, taste
grey clouds by blood red bushes.

LUCY WAKEFIELD

is currently completing her MLitt in Creative Writing at The University of Glasgow. Her writing is largely inspired by her childhood, relationships with her family, and the places they used to visit. Splitting her time between city life, her father's home and country living at her mother's, Wakefield often finds new inspirations from these surroundings and the parallels between the two.

236

CELL BLOCK 112

There is a jar of mayonnaise next to my bed.
I keep it there, because then I have an excuse to call you, and invite you round
because the lid is on too tight and I need it to
pop pop pop pop pop pop pop pop pop pop open for the chips I've let go cold, and soggy.
And I'll call you again in half an hour because my clipper won't
click click click click click click
and I can't light my seventh spliff of the day because I'm actually holding it upside-
down and the bud is spilling onto the leather of my desk chair.
In a couple of hours, I'll text you again and
tap tap tap tapping tap delete, tap up an excuse to see you.
I went with 'my lightbulb needs changing' which is true, but the one in the hall still
beams at me each morning.
I've managed to recall the exact pitch of your dial tone to
beeeeeeep...beep, beep, beep.
I don't bother leaving messages now,

I know you don't get them.

There's a bottle of ketchup in my bathroom.

Its Sainsbury's Basics label staring at the floor and sighing into a splodge of some
spilled toothpaste.

I keep it there for when you refuse to open the mayonnaise,

and I need a different condiment to drown myself in

because you've refused to come and see me because I'm being
juvenile and need to let it go.

But I don't think I can.

Because someone once told me that we rolled our cigarettes the same way, and we
laughed as you blew smoke rings into my clouds.

We would sit side by side,

your right leg crossed over your left,

elbow poised as you did the Sudoku and I mirrored you,
filling in the blanks you had left in the crossword.

We sat humming harmonies together and joking about starting a father-daughter
band.

It's been years since that sticky day,

and your tin still shuffles and

clinks clinks clinks clinks clinks

around in your pocket, cosying up to

your keys.

I'm grown now.
Older but still a shadow to your jumpers and woolly hats
that act as my carpet because I can't afford socks to warm the toes that I sadly
inherited from you.

I want to go back.
Back to the sofa bed in your lounge with the
vomit-stained quilt that you cover me in when we fall through the door from karaoke
night.

We never started our band, Dad.
You never learned to roll without a tin.
I still sit in your jumpers and thumb your woolly hats that have lost their fuzz. I sing
on my own now, with your voice in my lungs and your eyes on my back from behind
the bars
of cell block 112.

SARAH WALLIS

is a poet and playwright based
in Scotland. She holds an MA in Creative
Writing from UEA and an MPhil in Playwriting
from Birmingham University, as well as holding
theatrical residencies at Leeds Playhouse and
Harrogate Theatre. Wallis' work has appeared
in publications including *The Island Review, The
Interpreter's House, Selcouth Station, Ellipsis* and
Thimble.

THE PERSEPHONE ROOM

See the stucco walls in pale washed pink,
thin lines of trees raised up in silhouette
and dotted precious
with bright, gold, pomegranates,

spaced in time like planets, and set
to spin out the seasons of a hollow promise,
secret wedding banns posted,
the gold glinting and delicate balanced branches

seen by a candlelight set supper, ever a trick
to catch a girl on a darkling promise
of living in a different time,
another space, the room glimmers a threat

of change in the weather, shower of sparks
priming a cosy catch, romance spicing the dark.

And somewhere over and above adventuring,

the keen of a mother's six-month spaced grief.

A. M. WALSH

resides in Yorkshire. His poetry has
been published in various journals and
magazines in the UK and the US. He is the
author of the pamphlet *Flicker to a Burn*.

PETROLHEAD

Speed is the closest you can get to God without dying.
Wide eyed, head-to-the-back-of-your-seat, speed.
An oily oasis. The heart of a storm,
the sound of a choir in an empty cathedral.

Wide eyed, head-to-the-back-of-your-seat, speed.
Exhausts howl in insomniac tunnels, like
the sound of a choir in an empty cathedral,
with hymns echoing from pillars and arches.

Exhausts howl in insomniac tunnels, like
the choir in their empty cathedral,
with hymns echoing from pillars and arches.
Is it a coincidence that pews are arranged like cylinder blocks?

the choir in their empty cathedral,
an oily oasis. The heart of a storm,
is it a coincidence that pews are arranged like cylinder blocks?
Speed is the closest you can get to God without dying.

CAT WHITEHOUSE

was born and raised in London, UK, but currently calls South Korea home. As well as being a teacher and poet, she enjoys photography, embroidery and making the occasional appearance on Korean TV.

FOREST VIEW

The care home is surrounded by
A car park and a wrought iron fence;
Leafless litter scattered.
A cruel joke,
My grandmother would have said,
Five years ago.

Though even then,
She left the stove to burn all night,
And dropped her keys inside the kettle,
I would hear the metal jangle when
I went to pour us
A metallic cup of tea.

I didn't want to think of Forest View,
A backwoods of withered limbs,
Where nurses fed, washed, scolded,
And children
Left the home in tears,
Orphaned by the living.

So I dressed her like a Christmas tree,
Looped memories as tinsel,
Around her wizened trunk,
Hung ornaments of names and dates,
And strings of words,
As garlands of denial.

Until one day, the tree was bare,
But for the fairy sat atop,
Confused by how she'd gotten here,
So far from where the fairies play,

She asked me for a map and said,
She couldn't leave them waiting long.

I signed the papers, packed the bags,
And led the fairy through the trees,
Followed a trail of biscuit crumbs,
Down corridors to Room 15,
I left before the nurses came,
The guilt had made a ghost of me.

My grandmother sits in Forest View,
And names the flowers blooming
Where synapses once were.
Hibiscus, pansy, daisy,
She tells the other forest folk,
Bluebell, hyacinth, rose.

NATALIE WHITTAKER

lives in South East London, and is currently teaching at a secondary school, along with being a poet. She is the author of two pamphlets, *Shadow Dogs* and *Tree*, and her poems have been published in *Poetry News* and *The Valley Press Anthology of Prose Poetry*.

96

A chicken box ricochets down the aisle: *Hot
& Tasty — just the way you like it!* Tonight,
the pigeon-shit town washes by, under a cold
and tasteless sky; this place where we've wasted
our lives, like two spiders circling a sink.
And the plastic seats swing through the streets
and the STOP button shrieks at you to STOP,
but the silver trace of everyone's day has fogged
the top deck windows, and you dare to wipe
your name in the breath that's censed a hundred
rain-bedazzled hoods; knowing that the cost
of those letters in condensation — your
wet syllables ghosting sodium light —
is the use of all of those strangers' breaths.

PATRICK WILLAN

has previously worked as a journalist
and DJ in Ireland, before working as a teacher
in Ghana. He currently resides and works in
England. Willan's poetry explores themes such
as attachment and belonging; nature versus
avarice; and the force of music. His poems have
been published in *Havik, The Journal*, and he
is scheduled to be published in *Commonword's
Indivisible* anthology. www.patmellow.uk

COME COLLECT Y'ALL

You cannot believe seven words, eight bars
those hats still hold promise? Listen again
to delightful fly girl bringing her parsing:
debt collectors at my door. Insane

stabbed sass over her jay-oh-bee lover
meeting the gaze of a New York beauty
dubbed rent-seeking siren looking for other
guys to clock on and off but just not flee.

Wheel again this misery music, yes!
Echo the beats in your own chopped sound.
Prop up the aim of being the finest
to be awarded the belief of Gwen Guthrie, her highness.

SARAH WILLIS

is from Scotland, and she has previously
studied languages and literature at the
University of Edinburgh. She is currently
working on her first collection of poems
entitled *The Universe Sends Me Blossoms*.

THE SHIPS THAT SAIL THE SEAS

All those seas I've sailed.
All those ships I've passed in the night.
All those ships I've lost to storms.
All those sailors taken by the sirens and their songs.
All those seabirds squawking overhead.
All those sharks circling below.
All those swells I've navigated,
all those streams and undertows.
All those shores I've never reached.
All those shores I never will.
Captain of this ship,
across these seas I sail.

PATRICK WRIGHT

currently works at the Open University, where
he teaches English Literature and Creative
Writing, alongside working on a second PhD
in Creative Writing. He is the author of *Full
Sight Of Her* and his poems have been published
in magazines, including *Agenda*, *Wasafiri*, *The
Reader*, and *The High Window*. Wright's poem
'The End' appears in the *Best New British and Irish
Poets 2018* anthology, and he has previously been
shortlisted for the Bridport Prize.

BEFORE IT ALL STARTS UP

Outside from the Scarisbrick third floor window
a brass band takes a break down a ginnel.
There they clump, cups in hands. Now, as we
fold up our slacks, still half-inside our dreams,
I see the band salute, limbs of automata.
She can't be sure it's real, the line between

sleep and day more like a hinterland.
And now's such a time, where, before the maid
arrives, distracted from her rucksack,
she's enthralled by the show of light
splayed on walls through diamanté crystal.
I love how she dovetails one to the other,

how that dance of sunlight and soldiers is
choreographed. Such is the meaning she gives
to the morning, as I fall in love, again,
her mind gone 'quantum' (manic?), beyond
the band and businesses opening outside.
She makes sense of how it all knits together

as she lets a floral print frock fall down
her thighs, sprays lavender on the bit below
her collarbone. My eyes go to her fibula
or *fetlocks* as she calls them, as she passes me
the sun block, jushes my neck gaiter with forgotten
scent, my torso with protective witch hazel.
As usual we share her Clarins rose. Then she wonders
if the bouclé coat might go better, the weather as it is.

Here is happiness as the world filters in,
as the fan whirs on, in moments of just us

253

at the origin of things, before the drums
and horn start up again, before we're set to leave,
as she fashions a bandana out of lingerie,
when, forewarned by light, she wears a final skin.

LIST OF ANTHOLOGY POETS
SELECTED BY NICK MAKOHA

1) Peter Adair
2) Caroline Am Bergris
3) Alexandra Banister-Fletcher
4) Sarah Barr
5) Amy Blythe
6) Leo Boix
7) Caroline Bracken
8) Gavin Bradley
9) Michael A. Brown
10) Ian Cappelli
11) Simon Costello
12) Evan Costigan
13) A.M. Cousins
14) Elena Croitoru
15) Clive Donovan
16) Patrick James Errington
17) Rich Goodson
18) David Heidenstam
19) Maeve Henry
20) Johanna Higgins
21) Nyle Holihan
22) Patrick Holloway
23) Tamsin Hopkins
24) Thomas Irvine
25) Donald Jenkins
26) Dorothy Lawrenson
27) Katherine Lockton
28) Simon Maddrell
29) Raif Mansell
30) James McGovern
31) Sighle Meehan

32) Fred Melnyczuk
33) Audrey Molloy
34) Stephen James Moore
35) Beth Morrison
36) Oliver Mort
37) Kevin O'Keeffe
38) Mhairi Owens
39) Janet Philo
40) Yvonne Reddick
41) Sally Spedding
42) Alexandra Strnad
43) William Thompson
44) Peter Viggers
45) Sarah Wallis
46) A.M. Walsh
47) Natalie Whittaker
48) Sarah Willis
49) Patrick Wright

LIST OF ANTHOLOGY POETS
SELECTED BY AMIRA GHANIM

1) Muhibo Abdalla
2) Angela Arnold
3) Cynthia Asare-Dompreh
4) Robert Bal
5) Krystelle Bamford
6) Caroline Banerjee
7) Julie Bolitho
8) Jimmy Bowman
9) Terry Boyle
10) Matt Broomfield
11) Finn Cargill
12) Cate Carlow
13) Mark Chamberlain
14) Regi Claire
15) Charlotte Cornell
16) Kelly Davis
17) Emma Mahon Decker
18) Ege Dündar
19) Elio Escoffery
20) D.W. Evans
21) Roscanne Fahey
22) Rebecca Faulkner
23) Madison Fearn
24) Rebecca River Forbes
25) Tanatsei Gambura
26) Michael Glenfield
27) Maz Hedgehog
28) Daniel Hinds
29) Gloria Huwiler
30) Natasha Huynh

31) Joy James
32) Christopher M. James
33) Anna Rose James
34) Arun Jeetoo
35) Breda Joyce
36) Tom Kelly
37) Mirvat Manal
38) Marie Mayingi
39) Nicholas McGaughey
40) Andrew Geoffrey Kwabena Moss
41) D.M. O'Connor
42) Roua Oubira
43) Laura Potts
44) Cian Quinn
45) Guy Russell
46) Khanum Shaan
47) Neelam Shah
48) Lola Stansbury-Jones
49) Lucy Wakefield
50) Cat Whitehouse
51) Patrick Willan

AMIRA GHANIM

is a British Muslim editor,
writer and entrepreneur. She has a
background studying creative writing
and law, and has been Black Spring
Press Group's associate editor since
autumn 2019. She has read widely
in Middle Eastern poetry.

NICK MAKOHA's

debut collection *Kingdom
of Gravity* was shortlisted for the 2017
Felix Dennis Prize for Best First Collection
and nominated by *The Guardian* as one of
the best books of 2017. He was the 2019
Writer-in-Residence for The Wordsworth
Trust and Wasafiri.